PRAISE FOR CHRIS SCHWARTZ AND *RUFFHOUSE*

"Anyone who was paying attention in the '90s knows that Ruffhouse was one of the industry's 'it' labels, and looking back on that time now, it's easy to see why. In this fascinating and revealing book, Chris Schwartz describes how he went from hustling grimy Schoolly D records on the streets of Philadelphia to the pinnacle of mainstream success with Ms. Lauryn Hill, The Fugees, and Kris Kross. It's an absolute must-read for anybody who cares about hip-hop."
—BARRY WEISS,
partner and cofounder of Records,
LLC and longtime music industry veteran

"I've gotten to know Chris Schwartz very well over the past twenty-five years both personally and professionally, but there are elements to the Ruffhouse story that even I didn't know until I read this book. That's a testament to Chris and his abilities as a storyteller, and a reflection of his single-minded focus. If you loved *The Score* or *The Carnival*, you'll appreciate *Ruffhouse*." **—WYCLEF JEAN**

"From 'Jump' to 'Insane in the Brain' to 'Killing Me Softly,' Ruffhouse Records released some of the biggest hits of the 1990s and became, as a result of their meteoric rise, the talk of the industry. In this revealing and fascinating memoir, Chris Schwartz explains exactly how they did it, and then how it all came tumbling down. You could call it a cautionary tale, but that would be selling Chris's story short. Consider it instead a rare peek behind the curtain of a crazy business where stars and fortunes are instantly made and just as quickly unmade. I couldn't put it down." **—CHRIS BLACKWELL,** founder, Island Records

"In 1999, just six months after Ruffhouse artist Lauryn Hill snatched up all the Grammys, the label took a chance on me and put out my *Black Elvis/Lost in Space* concept album. Lauryn and I couldn't have been more different as artists, but that's one of the things that made the label great. They were able not only to produce a broad crossover smash like *The Miseducation of Lauryn Hill* but also to step out on a limb and push the creative envelope with a record like mine. Chris Schwartz is a true visionary, and I am grateful to him and his partner, Joe Nicolo, for their belief and support. Labels like Ruffhouse are few and far between today, and in this book Chris describes in vivid detail all the things, both positive and negative, that made them unique. It's a fascinating snapshot of a label's rise and ~~f-ll~~ ~~and all the crazy things~~ that contributed to both. It's a wild ride

T0125773

"[A] story of adversity and perseverance . . . Schwartz is strongest when describing the creative process and most fascinating when revealing the difficult decisions that go into each production and release. He is celebratory when success is attained and honest when an outcome is less than he'd hoped for . . . Fans of these artists will love the insider information on the recording process and the trials and tribulations of getting this music out into the world." **−LIBRARY JOURNAL**

"Recounts a pivotal era in Philly music history. Even more gripping: his personal tale of surviving a violent home life on the Main Line to become a top Philly producer." **−PHILADELPHIA MAGAZINE**

"A revealing and fascinating memoir . . . If you want a real inside look at the music business, this story is filled with the good times and disasters." **−WMGK RADIO**

"Detail[s] not only the good and bad times of rap and rock, but what it meant to be digging in the trenches, mired in the struggle to make hit records." **−PHILADELPHIA WEEKLY**

"The book is a work of truly stunning revelation. Not just because it details the inner sanctum of a world (the recording industry) whose hidden machinations have changed little between the old days and the present . . . But, how tortured minds could triumph over adversity to find themselves and their lives calling . . . Schwartz is a quickly paced and colorful writer who knows how to keep the action coming and the anecdotes tightly packed and crisply compacted for maximum drama." **−DOSAGE MAGAZINE**

"For serious fans of 1990s hip-hop music and for those interested in the lives of music-industry veterans, *Ruffhouse* is a quick read." **−POPMATTERS**

"The book chronicles Ruffhouse's rise in the pre-Napster era when the music industry was making money hand over fist . . . *Ruffhouse* tells tales of those mega-selling acts, and many compelling characters . . . But *Ruffhouse* also has a different, intensely personal story to tell." **−PHILADELPHIA INQUIRER**

"Impressively candid and exceptionally informative." **−MIDWEST BOOK REVIEW**

"A collection of entertaining streetwise stories from the '90s—back when the music industry sold physical product, indie labels were on the rise, and a smart young guy with an ear for new music and a head for business could charge onto the Billboard charts."
—*MILWAUKEE SHEPHERD EXPRESS*

"Schwartz's memoir, *Ruffhouse*, is full of funny, wild, and insightful anecdotes detailing his years building one of the world's biggest rap labels."
—OKAYPLAYER

"*Ruffhouse* reveals an insider's perspective of record companies, recording, touring, and the heights of hip-hop's 1990s heyday. *Ruffhouse* is a great read. It offers an examination of hip-hop culture as it transformed into a worldwide commercial monolith."
—DIRTY GLOVE BASTARD

"It was a small outfit that made a big impact, and *Ruffhouse* tells the story of that record label that organically grew from production and artist management to one of the most successful independent hip-hop houses of the 1990s . . . A memoir of the rise of Ruffhouse and the changing economics and environment of the music business over that time . . . The book's biggest strength aside from its raw honesty is the amount of information and education Schwartz gives in terms of the way the music industry operates and how the large labels conduct their businesses."
—*THE PASSION OF CHRISTOPHER PIERZNIK*

RUFF HOUSE

FROM THE STREETS OF PHILLY TO THE
TOP OF THE '90S HIP-HOP CHARTS

CHRIS SCHWARTZ

DIVERSION
BOOKS

For more information, email info@diversionbooks.com

Diversion Books
A division of Diversion Publishing Corp.
443 Park Avenue South, suite 1004
New York, NY 10016
www.diversionbooks.com

First Diversion Books paperback edition July 2020
Paperback ISBN: 978-1-63576-730-8
eBook ISBN: 978-1-63576-597-7

Printed in The United States of America

1 3 5 7 9 10 8 6 4 2

Library of Congress cataloging-in-publication data is available on file.

For Myrna and Ava

CONTENTS

FOREWORD

MY CONNECTION TO Ruffhouse Records has complete disregard for chronological order. This has mainly to do with the fact that Chris Schwartz and I spoke infrequently when I was a Fugee, spoke more during *The Miseducation of Lauryn Hill*, but really didn't become close until after all of that happened.

By that time, Ruffhouse was no longer and I had left fame and celebrity behind for what I referred to as a "wilderness" period. It was during this time that my conversations with Chris transcended the basic banter and mystery that typically went on between artists and record company owners. I had developed a disdain for the process, for both some of the "show" and some of the "business," and could really only tolerate communicating with people who were beyond it.

Chris reached out to me one day and I spoke aggressively, in a manner unlike I had ever communicated with him before. I recounted a history that had moved so fast that some parts of it seemed like a blur. Some parts were music history legend, others were hilarious, and yet others provoked rage and at times genuine sadness within me. We started to strip the layers of veneer from our relationship and how we expressed ourselves to each other. He listened to my anger and did his best to make room for it. After all, I was a teenager when I signed my first record deal and had given a large portion of my up-until-then life to the grind that made corporate institutions filthy with money and established a rich foundation upon which they would promote the seemingly similar artists who followed after me. I didn't feel properly appreciated, understood, or supported, and for a period Chris was one of the only people I could express that feeling to.

He, too, had a story, filled with both great memories and some discontent. We shared, listened, laughed, analyzed, and developed a compassion and understanding for each other that neither one of us probably expected to cultivate. It was at this time that I learned about him, his background, upbringing, early grind, how Ruffhouse came to be, and what it all meant to him. I was in a place of hyper self-analysis and couldn't help but draw parallels between the stories of his childhood and what would eventually happen with Ruffhouse. Even now, the name seems like a metaphor.

I am grateful to Chris Schwartz for having the vision to recognize my talent and the fortitude to believe in it. This book tells that story and so much more.

Ms. Lauryn Hill
February 2019

INTRODUCTION

I KNEW ABOUT the people involved with Ruffhouse before I knew about Ruffhouse. I knew about Chris Schwartz, who started out as a guitar player and drum programmer—he got his hands on an 808 back in the early '80s, when drum machines were bridging the gap between international prog and electronics and American soul and then hip-hop. If the rumors are to be believed, he had his 808 even before Marvin Gaye recorded "Sexual Healing." And I knew about Joe "The Butcher" Nicolo, of course, who had founded Studio 4 with his brother, Phil, and was already making his name as a producer in both pop music (Billy Joel), underground rock (Urge Overkill), and Philly hip-hop (Robbie B & Jazzy J "Rock The Go-Go!").

The two of them came together around Schoolly D, the godfather of gangster rap. Chris was managing him, and Joe had produced some early sessions for him, both in Philly and elsewhere. In the late '80s, Chris and Joe joined forces to found Ruffhouse Records, in a joint venture with Columbia Records.

One of their first breakout acts came not from Philly, but from Georgia, in the form of two little kids who were discovered in a shopping mall by Jermaine Dupri. Those kids became Kris Kross, and then became stars.

Right around that time, Ruffhouse picked up another hip-hop talent: me. But they didn't get me as a drummer or a band, because I wasn't quite one of those yet. Instead, they got me as an intern. As luck—or fate—would have it, I attended the ceremony for the Philadelphia Music Alliance's Walk of Fame because my father, Lee Andrews, was being inducted for his career as a doo-wop and soul pioneer. At the time, I was working for an insurance company, but I was itching to get out of there and use my spare time to work on music. At the ceremony, I explained that to a woman who happened to work at Ruffhouse, and she offered me an internship on the spot.

At Ruffhouse, I kept my head down. I didn't tell them that I had designs on stardom, or even on a music career. I had another objective entirely, which was to learn the record business. And that I did. This was back in the old days, when instead of just tap-tap-tapping an album name into a SoundScan database, record labels had to call around to local stores to see how many units they had moved. I got street-level experience that way. I saw how the sausage was made and sometimes how it was unmade. It was an invaluable experience.

Later on, when the Roots coalesced, one of the first groups we opened for was a Ruffhouse group, The Goats, who made hard-charging political rap music, including one fantastically ambitious record (*Tricks of the Shade*). And Chris Schwartz wrote me a check for $2,000 that helped for the "Pass the Popcorn" video from *Organix*, the Roots' first album. You can call it a gift, or a reward for two years of free labor, but at the time it felt like the Mean Joe Greene Coke commercial, when Joe threw his jersey to a kid in the tunnel. Thanks, Mean Joe!

Ahmir "Questlove" Thompson
February 2019

PROLOGUE

I DROPPED OUT of the opening in the dressing room wall and landed on top of the dumpster, startling some of the clubgoers who'd stepped outside to smoke some weed. Through the wall behind me I could hear the bouncers still banging on the dressing room door that I'd just been trapped behind. I brushed myself off and scanned the parking lot, but Schoolly's Lincoln Continental was nowhere to be seen. Shit. Did he really just leave me stranded in a New Jersey club parking lot surrounded by a crazed mob? The bouncers' voices got louder; it was only a matter of minutes before they'd bust down that door. I had to get out of here.

"You're bleeding," a girl said to me as I rushed past the club entrance, jetting by the upset crowd demanding their money back from the manager. I ignored the girl, closed my jean jacket, and walked out into the street, dodging traffic. I must have cut myself climbing out of the building, but that wasn't important right now. I had to find Schoolly. Besides, blood didn't bother me, nor did broken bones. Although I would prefer to avoid getting beat down by a group of Jersey club bouncers, it would not be the first time. Brutality and I go way back. When it comes to violence, I was home schooled.

CHAPTER ONE

FRACTURED FAIRY TALES

t wasn't really an accident, but that's what everyone called it. That's how it was explained to doctors in the emergency room and to neighbors, teachers, school officials, and family friends—anybody who was curious about the mishaps I suffered at the hands of my older brothers. The real reason was never spoken of. I could usually anticipate when an "accident" would occur—from a bad mood or a night of too many drinks. But I did not see this one coming.

My family's home sat under a flight path for military aircraft, so I frequently gazed at the sky watching C-130s, P-3s, helicopters, and all manner of military aircraft. I stood on the front lawn looking at the sky, daydreaming as I often did. Suddenly, something hit me so hard that it ripped the air from my lungs. My eight-year-old body twisted around at an unnatural angle; my right hipbone ripped from its socket and a tendon tore on my left knee. My right leg hung limp with the foot facing inward, totally flat in the wrong direction. My left knee swelled to the size of a softball. My head hit the ground so hard the world looked like a grainy Super 8 with no sound. I looked up to see my brother, John, standing over me, legs spread with one foot on each side of my prone body yelling something unintelligible. I regained my breath as the agonizing pain from my injuries came on full throttle. Once I found my voice, I screamed in agony.

"You just need to walk it off." John laughed it off, calling me a pussy before he walked into the house. I screamed at the top of my lungs at my parents' bedroom window, just above us, hoping to get my mother's attention. The curtains were drawn. She usually locked herself away in the bedroom in one of her combination alcohol-tranquilizer cocoons.

I could not move my legs. I laid there screaming and gasping, hoping somebody might hear me, but no one did. I thought I would die. I rolled my body over and crawled, using my arms to drag myself to the house about thirty feet away. Every little movement was pure agony. It took me a good while to make it to the porch. Finally, the door opened, and my mother, in her slurred voice, wanted to know what was going on.

John bellowed in the background from within the house, "He's faking it."

My mother slammed the door shut. She did not want to be bothered. I laid there half on the porch and half on the front walk for what seemed an eternity. Finally, a car pulled in our driveway. It was my father returning from being on the road all day visiting retail furniture accounts.

As he came upon me, the front door opened, and John said sheepishly, "We were playing football."

My leg lay twisted, and I had pissed my pants. That's all my father needed to see. He carried me to the backseat of his car and drove to the emergency room. I vomited all over myself. A nurse asked me to take deep breaths, but my head exploded every time I looked at a fluorescent light.

A doctor examined the back of my head and shone a penlight in my eyes. He told my father I most likely had a concussion. They carefully took off my clothes, which by then were drenched in urine and covered with vomit. They X-rayed me and then put me under. I woke up in traction with my right leg suspended by a wire counterbalanced with weights. They had set my hip while I was under and had my left knee wrapped and propped on a cushion. I stayed like that for two days while the doctors scheduled me for a body cast. The application of the cast was as painful as the tackle.

In a tiled room, the doctors pointed to a table with a pole fixed in the middle of the table top about two inches in diameter and eighteen inches high. At the top of this pole was a piece of metal four inches long and one inch wide. They told me they needed me to straddle it. About six or seven people, nurses, doctors, and orderlies, lifted me from my bed to the table and placed me on this piece of metal while they supported my legs, arms, and head. The doctors first wrapped me from the neck down in cotton gauze, like a mummy. It took them about an hour and a half to wrap me in plaster. The cast went from chest level at my armpits all the way down to my right foot, leaving the toes and my leg below my left knee exposed. They attached a piece of wood across my knees to stabilize it and keep the plaster secure.

I spent several months in the body cast. I missed almost all of third grade and did not walk again for nearly a year. Amazingly, my school graduated me to the next grade, even though I missed all that time in school. My parents visited me occasionally at the hospital, but it was the nuns from my school who visited me the most. They brought me little gifts and get-well cards from my classmates.

The nuns stood around my hospital bed telling me corny jokes, singing songs, and praying. The nuns, oblivious of the real circumstances behind my accident, were very nice. Everybody was told I was playing football. It made sense, of course; I came from a football family of seven boys and three girls. The boys, with the exception of myself, were all of exceptionally large stature. My brothers were all football players of note. The story was plausible. Except it had one small, unmentioned technicality: there was no actual football.

"He has brittle bones," they'd explain away my latest injury, like it was an actual diagnosed physical impairment. After my hospital stay, I was transported back to our house in an ambulance. My father rented a hospital bed that was set up in our downstairs den, being too big to put anywhere else in the house. My grandmother, a no-nonsense matron, came over to visit while everybody was at school. I could hear her talking with my father in the living room. She did not pull her punches:

"John should be severely punished."

I listened keenly to hear my father's reply. There was none.

To the outside world, we were a large, rowdy German-Irish Catholic family. But there was a frightening dynamic—a deep-rooted hostility among three of my older brothers—George, Kevin, and John—and their assaults on me were no more than an inconvenience to my parents. My mother often locked herself away in her bedroom, and my father, a traveling furniture salesman, was always on the road to support his ten kids.

The origins of my brothers' behaviors are a mystery to me even to this day. Nothing came up in my family's history. My great-great-grandfather, Valentine Schwartz, a cabinetmaker, came over from Germany in the 1800s, along with the thousands of German craftsmen who settled in New York, Ohio, and Pennsylvania. Valentine set up a cabinet shop in Lehighton, Pennsylvania, to make cabinets, coffins, and household furniture items for coal miners. The cabinet shop also doubled as a funeral home and, later on, became a furniture store run by Valentine's sons and grandsons. My father, George A. Schwartz, trained as an Army Air-Corps B-24 Bombardier, stationed in the South Pacific during World War II. After that, he fell into the family business and became a furniture salesman.

My father met my mother, Lois Knapp, on a blind date in New York City. She was the eldest of Elwin Knapp's four daughters. Elwin Knapp and his brother, Clarence, ran their own business selling discount Navy surplus shoes, employing door-to-door sales people. The company's success led to the launch of their own manufacturing company in Brockton, Massachusetts, which, at one time, was among the largest manufacturers of work shoes in the United States.

Elwin was a wealthy man, but later in his life, he took a second, younger wife. Consequently, none of his fortune ever made it to our generation. As a result, my father worked incredibly hard to support the family.

As is the custom of devout Roman Catholics, my parents set about having a large brood of children. Our family is made up of two distinct sets of siblings: the older brothers and sisters, going from oldest to youngest (George, Marguerite, Robert, Kevin, and John), and the younger group, going oldest to youngest (Ann, myself, Karl, Paul, and Beth). We lived in

various homes in Massachusetts and Pennsylvania before set-
tling in Devon, Pennsylvania, when I was five years old. The
house sat in a development surrounded by farmlands and old
industrial-era estates in an area outside Philadelphia known as
"The Main Line," named after the Pennsylvania Railroad designation for the commuter rail between Philadelphia and
Lancaster.

I was born on December 27, 1960 at Jefferson Hospital in
Philadelphia. Shortly after my birth—and still with no name—I
contracted pneumonia and was not expected to live. My father
baptized me in a sink at the hospital as my condition deterio-
rated. But, miraculously, I survived. Dr. Alison was credited
with saving my life. In homage to him, I was named Alison
Christopher Schwartz. Sometime in my early childhood, I
started using my middle name, Christopher, as my first name.

I attended Saint Monica's School in Berwyn, the town over
from Devon, from first to sixth grade, with a short stint in public elementary school in fifth grade. While in public school, I
was bullied by other kids for having a prominent lisp. School
officials enlisted a speech therapist to help. The lisp stayed
with me until I eventually lost most of it by the time I was
seventeen.

My father worked long hours. He traveled daily, visiting retail accounts selling high-end furniture throughout the
mid-Atlantic and parts of the Northeast. He committed to
making sure we had food on the table. He left the house early
in the morning and did not return until late at night. Whenever he was home, he either watched Notre Dame football or
read his spy novels. An avid reader, he loved books about
World War II espionage.

Motherhood wore on my mother, and the toll of taking care
of ten kids, ranging in age from infants to teenagers, left her

turning to alcohol. My parents were definitely of the cocktail generation, and by the time the younger group of kids in our family were of school age, my mother turned to alcohol as numbing medication. Her doctors frequently prescribed Thorazine and Lithium—staple tools of the psychiatric profession in the '60s and '70s. My mother would be institutionalized for short periods leaving my father having to hire people to look after us. Her condition made her incapable of doing anything for us.

The absence of my father and the inability of my mother to cope with reality created a *Lord of the Flies* dynamic within the family. The lack of parental supervision left some of my brothers to terrorize the neighborhood. The police were frequently visitors to our home, and the neighbors generally considered us to be white trash. In part due to my smaller stature, lack of interest in sports, and my intellect, and in part for reasons I still cannot explain, I was a favorite target for George Jr., Kevin, and John, who were prone to violence. While my younger siblings were, mostly, immune to the abuse, I was frequently the victim of unprovoked assaults. Kevin, in particular, had carte blanche to commit violence unabated. He fashioned himself a surrogate disciplinarian as some kind of demented justification. He took advantage of my father's absence to create an atmosphere of terror.

Kevin used violence as a way to make his life carefree and comfortable; he was lazy, ignorant, and selfish. If he wanted a glass of milk while watching TV, he expected it to be brought to him. We did his laundry, cleaned his room, washed his car. We were there to serve his every need under the threat of violence. We were not allowed to talk in his presence. We sat there at the dinner table in frightened silence while he glowered; he enjoyed watching us react in fear, particularly when he'd raise his hand and pretend to strike us.

One winter, I needed a coat. My mother, being too inebriated to take me to get one, gave Kevin money to take me to buy one. But at the store he tried on coats for himself until he found the perfect ski coat. He then handed it to me and told me to try it on. The coat was so big it hung down below my knees. He paid for the coat, and we went home. I did not dare to protest. I never wore that ridiculously oversized coat, and I froze my ass off that winter wearing an old corduroy coat with the lining ripped out. But at least Kevin had a coat to wear skiing even though nobody in my family skied. It was considered an activity for rich people.

The disparity in age between the two sets of siblings was enough that when my oldest brother, George Jr., came home from college to start his first job, I was not sure who he was. I had no real memories of him before he left for school. George appeared one morning—some guy with bushy blond hair and a scraggly beard—at the top of the stairs talking to my mother while I stood behind her wondering who this stranger was and why he was so familiar with my mother. He was starting a new job in construction in Philadelphia, so he moved back in to our already crowded house.

George Jr. saw the younger set of siblings as an inconvenience and referred to us loudly as "the little cocksuckers" who he routinely brutalized. Shortly after he came home to live with us, I discovered a baseball card collection in the attic and sat at the top of the third-floor landing sorting them. I had no idea who they belonged to. It was a pretty big collection, filling a number of shoeboxes. George Jr. came home from work and, when he discovered me with his baseball cards, threw me down a flight of stairs.

George Jr. didn't need even that much justification to commit violence. He would come home after work and ask my mother, "Who gave you the hardest time today?"

It was his way of justifying his favorite after-work activity. My mother made a feeble attempt to say we were all well behaved, but he ignored her, dragging me down to the basement. He locked the basement door and tied my wrists to a support pole. He then repeatedly hit me with a belt or a golf club while he drank his quart of Miller beer. This was his way of blowing off steam after a day of construction work. The day he moved out of the house for good was one of the most joyous days I can remember. But the physical assaults were not behind me as Kevin and John remained in the house.

I slept on a bunk bed in a room with my brothers, Karl and Paul. One morning, I was asleep on the top bunk when I was suddenly pulled out of the bed by my legs. My body crashed down onto the tiled floor, disorienting me. Kevin stood over me, punching me relentlessly. I tried fruitlessly to scramble away into the laundry room, but he pinned me down and climbed on top of me. He grabbed my head and started slamming it on the tile floor. My father heard the commotion, ran down from the kitchen, and tried to pull him off of me, but Kevin was too strong. My father retrieved a kitchen knife and stabbed Kevin in the side. Kevin laid there on his side, groaning, while my mother, awoken by the madness, screamed at my father. In that moment, I hoped Kevin would die. But, alas, the wound was not deep, and Kevin recovered.

But it was the youngest of my older brothers, John, who took things to a new level.

One Sunday morning, John woke up and announced to us that since our activities were loud and deprived him of being able to sleep in, he was going to put us to work. This was usually something Kevin would do, but since Kevin was not home, John thought he would try it out.

I said no and took off up the stairs. He ran after me, and when he caught up with me, he grabbed me from behind, pulled me down, and kicked me in the head. I blacked out.

My next memory was waking up in John's bed covered in vomit.

My younger brother, Karl, told me I had been there for two days. I was dizzy, my head splitting. I did not remember how I got into John's bed or why. My head hurt so much I could only lay there in the dark.

Any rational person either would have called an ambulance or at least taken me to a hospital, but for some reason John took me to his room on the third floor. At the end of the second day, when my condition showed little to no improvement, he bought me a little packet of aspirin as a pathetic attempt to try to fix the situation. Luckily for John and me, I did eventually recover.

Of the three brothers, John was the one I never wanted to be alone in the house with. When I was thirteen, he tied my wrists behind my back with copper wire and kneeled on my chest, beating my face, breaking my nose and teeth. There was nobody at home, and I could only do one thing: ask for mercy. It only provoked him.

"Mercy? You want mercy?" he sputtered, his face dark red and eyes glazed. A glob of spit hung from the side of his mouth.

The punches came nonstop. I thought he was going to kill me. Getting punched in the face repeatedly with your hands tied behind your back is not like in the movies where the victim makes witty remarks while being assaulted. It's a horrific, terrifying experience. Mentally, I went to another place. I could not feel the blows, but I could hear them.

Then my world went dark.

I don't recall how much time passed before I was able to hobble to the bathroom to look at my almost unrecognizable face. That's when John happened by and said casually, "Every time it hurts, think of me."

I went to school with a swollen, disfigured face, complete with two black eyes, one eye swollen shut, a broken nose, and my lips grossly puffed out. I walked through the halls keeping my head down as other kids looked at me with alarmed curiosity. People at school were used to me showing up with a black eye or bruises, but this was ugly. I only felt embarrassment and shame, like I was some pathetic outcast to be looked down upon.

A group of male teachers, unsatisfied with my routine explanation that I was injured "playing football," enlisted my sister, Ann, to find out the truth. After, they paid John a visit at his work. I was never told what had transpired, but it didn't change anything. I cannot recall having one meal at our kitchen table that did not involve John transmitting threats to me across the table.

The constant physical abuse from my brothers was enough to make me consider ways out. But then there was a new element added to their repertoire of verbal torments. My six brothers were all physically big guys and athletic. I had a normal stature and wasn't much for sports. Instead, I enjoyed an advanced reading curriculum in school and loved music. As a result, in 1973, when I was in seventh grade, Kevin decided I must be gay and made his proclamations known to all. He would bellow in his Fred Flintstone voice, "I am telling you, he is a fucking queer!" He was successful in convincing my mother of this, and he even had my father giving me questionable looks.

And even my nicer siblings inquired. One day, while driving with Robert, he said, "I know what everybody is saying about you, and I just want you to know it's okay with me." I was so surprised at this pronouncement, I did not respond. Instead, my hatred for George Jr., Kevin, and John continued to grow. I was not gay, but my violent, sociopathic, homophobic brothers continued with the verbal torments.

On more than one occasion, I considered suicide, but I could not work up the courage. Running away seemed easier. I once ran away as far as Maryland, but the other kid I was with bragged to a girl working at a McDonald's about us running away, and the workers called the police.

In ninth grade, I considered joining the merchant marine apprentice program in Maryland. I was looking for any opportunity get away from those assholes. I was looking at brochures for the merchant marines one day at the kitchen table when Kevin remarked, "Yeah, if you try any of your faggot stuff there, they will throw you right out." Comments like these made me fantasize about cutting his throat. My hand reached for a steak knife, and I was suddenly overtaken by a desire to turn around and bury it in his stomach, but I didn't have the nerve.

Through all of the craziness in my family, one constant rang true throughout my childhood: music. It became my only escape from a miserable existence and ultimately brought me close friendships.

Due to the difference in the age of my brothers and older sisters, I was introduced to a lot of music at a very early age. From the time I was just a baby, there was different music coming from different rooms in my house. Throughout my early years as a child of the sixties, I grew up on the popular music on Philadelphia's WFIL AM radio, as well as lot of the FM album rock coming from Philadelphia's WMMR, one the first FM progressive rock stations in the country. I loved the Beatles and grew up believing popular music started and ended with them. The Beatles were my go-to, but I liked other artists, too: Bob Dylan, the Grateful Dead, Electric Light Orchestra, Led Zeppelin, James Brown, Jimi Hendrix, Cream, Bob Marley, Eric Clapton, Pink Floyd, the Rolling Stones, the Allman Brothers. I developed a penchant for Frank Zappa in junior high because I was drawn to the complexity of the arrangements and his guitar playing. Later, I developed an addiction for jazz fusion groups, like Weather Report, Mahavishnu Orchestra, Return to Forever, and Jean-Luc Ponty.

I did not have a stereo, but I bought an old phonograph at a church flea market that lasted a remarkable number of years. I often carried a portable cassette player with me, but it went through batteries faster than I could keep up. My brothers had tons of records, but you only needed to get your fingers broken once to know that their records and stereos were off-limits.

When I was nine, I bought a guitar at the Saint David's Fair flea market and taught myself how to play a few chords. It was an old Sears Silvertone acoustic guitar, which lasted about a month and a half before it was broken. I could never own anything of value or importance. I fantasized about having my own guitar and amplifier in my own bedroom where I could play uninterrupted for as long as I liked, like other kids I knew had. I had read a story about Eric Clapton secluding himself in an apartment for two years doing nothing but playing guitar. That sounded to me like utopia. Artistic pursuits were looked upon with disdain by certain family members. I thought if I had the opportunity, I could become a great guitar player and start a band, but my home life was so transient. I got my first job at thirteen washing dishes at a banquet house called the Bella Villa. I would operate the big dishwashing machine, and while scrubbing pots and pans, I would stand on old wooden Coca-Cola crates wearing a Phillies batting helmet so the pots and pans wouldn't fall on me when I hung them up. When I received my first check, I went to the Wayne Music store and bought myself an electric guitar—a used Penco imitation Gibson SG. My father thought it foolish, saying, "Why don't you get yourself some clothes?" Although I wore mostly hand-me-downs that were several sizes too big, I didn't care. I wanted this guitar in the worst way. I learned a few songs by Cream, Bob Dylan, and the Allman Brothers. Not well enough to play them in a band, but it was a start. The guitar was a little beat up, so I took it to woodshop at school and refinished it. I stripped it, sanded it down, and stained it. I thought it was beautiful. Within three weeks I came home to find it broken beyond repair.

My only means of avoiding physical assaults by my older brothers was to not go home. I never came home after school until it was very late at night. When I came home at night, I felt the hoods and radiators of my brothers' cars to see if they were still warm. Depending on how warm they felt, I knew if they just got home and would still be up. I'd grab a plastic lawn chair and sit in the woods and wait, sometimes for hours, until I thought they were asleep. I then snuck into the house through the downstairs den. On weekends and in the summer, I got up at five or six in the morning to get out of the house before the assholes were awake, and I stayed away until dark.

Staying away from home was not easy, especially since I never had any money. I spent a lot of time at the homes of my two closest friends. I also spent a good part of my childhood working on a farm in Villanova, Pennsylvania. It was a place that my brothers never knew about where I could go to get away. Ardrossan Farms was a dairy operation that was part of a large estate. It was about three miles from my house, and I worked there with my best friend, Terry Akins. Terry was like a surrogate brother, a friend since the second grade. We were inseparable. Terry's father was a successful stockbroker, and the family was well off. His house became my second home— or better yet, it became my first home.

It was hard not to look at other families and wonder why they seemed so normal and my family seemed so fucked up. I made a few attempts to try to do things that other kids did. I joined the Cub Scouts in fourth grade. I was very proud of my new uniform, and I was wearing it at dinner one night for a Scout meeting after. That night, my face got slammed into a bowl of soup that ended up all over my new uniform. I did not go to the Cub Scouts meeting; instead, I quit.

In seventh grade art class, I met and bonded over Frank Zappa records with my classmate, Jeff Coulter, who remains one of my best friends to this day. Jeff was a quiet guy who had lost his oldest brother in a car accident, and I knew he had gone through some rough times. Jeff and I both had similar tastes in music, and he played drums. Jeff's wonderful mother welcomed me into their home. When my buddy, Terry, moved up to Boston with his mother, Jeff's house became my sanctuary.

By the time I was in tenth grade, it was clear that I needed to get away from this eternal nightmare. I knew I had no chance of finishing school. I had stopped going to class as my low self-esteem and lisp made me a bully magnet. I was lambasted by family members over letters from school detailing my absences. The school did not understand how I could score in the top percentile on their tests and, yet, not go to class. The school had a psychologist examine me. My mother lied to the school, telling them I was under psychiatric treatment for emotional issues. It was another lie invented to draw away attention from the House of Horrors. She dressed it up quite nicely, and based on her fabrications, school officials decided I would be better served going to a school at Embreeville State Hospital, a mental institution in Chester County. I took a daily one-hour bus ride there by myself with no other kids on the bus.

Embreeville State Hospital looked ominous, surrounded by chain link fencing with rolls of razor wire on top. Several stand-alone buildings were scattered throughout the campus. It was right out of *The Shawshank Redemption*. Patients walked around in bathrobes, talking to themselves. Classes were held in the wing of one of the buildings. I was the youngest student there, and the other students gave me cause to be concerned. I knew I did not belong there.

After one week at the school, an argument broke out between two kids during class. Suddenly, one kid with a knife lunged across my desk at another kid, cutting his hand and shoulder open. Blood ended up on my face and clothes. That was it. I never went back. I spent the rest of that winter wandering the streets, waiting until I turned seventeen.

A few days before my seventeenth birthday, I went to the Armed Forces recruitment office on Broad Street in Philadelphia and talked to different recruiters. The Army, Marines, and Air Force all had boot camps starting two months after enlistment date. I did not want to wait that long—I could not wait that long. The Navy offered a boot camp two weeks after enlistment date. So I joined the Navy. I left the recruiting station knowing that those two weeks would be the longest in my life.

You could join the military at seventeen, but you needed parental consent. That was easy enough for me to get. All I had to do was lift my mother's hand and have her sign the papers while she was passed out.

The day I left for the Navy, I went to the recruiter's office. Recruits for all branches of the service were taken into a room to be sworn in together. After we swore the oath, somebody asked one of the recruiters if they could go outside for a cigarette.

"No!" the recruiter snapped. "You will not do anything unless you are told to!"

All the recruits were taken aback at this command, perhaps some a little regretful of their decision.

I was thrilled. Nothing could be as bad as it was at home.

CHAPTER TWO

HAZE GRAY AND UNDERWAY

n January of 1978, I flew from Philadelphia to Orlando, Florida, for Navy boot camp. It was my first airplane trip. At the airport, sitting amongst the other fresh recruits, I examined my peers. Most of the guys were young, late teens to early twenties. For the most part, they appeared like stragglers coming from their last high school keg party. Young men of limited prospects like myself, who chose the military as an alternative to an hourly wage vocation. I had just turned seventeen a few days before; I was pretty sure I was the youngest recruit.

Most of the group had arrived at the airport drunk, stoned, and unrepentant. And most spent the three hours before the flight took off at the airport bar drinking. I was not old enough to drink, and I was too shy to add to the conversation, so I quietly sat by myself.

They were loud and boisterous, telling jokes and stories, a few which involved joining the military as a condition of avoiding incarceration. Others talked about being dumped by girlfriends, fired from jobs they hated, or just wanting to get away to have an adventure.

The evening flight landed us in Orlando around one in the morning. Navy petty officers met our plane. As we walked—and some stumbled, still drunk—through the arrival doors to the outside, I was engulfed by warm humid air, sticky against my skin. Palm trees, like the ones I'd seen on *Gilligan's Island*, bordered the doorway. This felt like another country, 1500 glorious miles from my childhood House of Horrors. Gray school buses escorted us to the Naval base where we were directed into a building to be issued black raincoats, which we were told to put on. Our group was herded into a temporary barracks outfitted with bunk beds with bare mattresses.

We each claimed a bunk, using our raincoats as blankets. After lights out, I thought about my situation, lying there in the dark amongst fifty other guys sleeping in raincoats. For the first time since I could remember, I didn't have to think about the next day, worrying about what it would bring or what could happen to me. For what seemed like the first time in my life I could go to sleep and dream.

At daybreak, we received regulation haircuts and uniforms and were assigned to our training units. Music was a great conversational denominator. I could banter with any of these guys from anywhere, white or African-American. The Navy had boot camps in Orlando, San Diego, and Great Lakes, Michigan. They send recruits to the training units closest to where they are from. Normally, I would have been sent to Great Lakes but ended up in Orlando with a small contingent of other guys from the Northeast. The majority of the guys in our unit were from the South. Some of them from very remote, rural areas. Until then, I had never met someone who only owned one pair of shoes. I was still very shy, but I started to learn how to talk and converse with confidence. I wasn't bullied, ostracized, or disparaged. I found something out about myself, that given the circumstances I could actually be funny and entertaining. Navy boot camp is not like the other branches of the military. There is marching, inspections, drilling, and physical training, but that is where the similarity ends. Where the other branches train for combat and weapons, the Navy teaches you to live on a ship where everybody has a dual job responsibility. Besides your chosen occupation, be it a gunner's mate, cook, sonar technician, navigator, helmsman, boatswain's mate, or any of the multitude of positions required for operations, every sailor and officer is also assigned a designated collateral responsibility in the event of battle or fire. Fires are bad news at sea and are a given during a battle if the ship get struck by enemy armament. Ship compartments have interlocking water-tight doors and hatches. If the ship gets torpedoed or bombed, the compartments get flooded and need to be pumped out to maintain the ship's structural integrity. These activities are carried out with a choreographed execution involving every person on board and are constantly drilled.

During boot camp, I was made the guide-on bearer, meaning I carried the flag bearing the unit's insignia when we marched in formation. Perhaps I was given this position due to my terrible posture (in part due to my low self-esteem), and the Chief Petty Officers felt a role where one had to keep his shoulders back to properly carry the flag would be perfect to help with my posture. Not that it did much good.

My twelve weeks of boot camp flew by, and it was time for me to jump into my next job. When I enlisted, I had signed up to go into aviation. I had mistakenly thought they said I would be doing aviation "ordinance." I took that to mean compliance in regard to Naval aircraft. I'd pictured myself walking around with a clipboard inspecting fighter jets. I could not have been more mistaken.

The word I misconstrued as ordinance was actually "ordnance," as in bombs, rockets, guns, and missiles. At the end of boot camp, I was assigned to load jets with all sorts of destructive devices. I did not have any feelings about it one way or another, except when they told me I was going to Memphis, Tennessee, for my training.

I could not have been more thrilled. Memphis, where Elvis Presley, Aretha Franklin, Otis Redding, Johnny Cash, B.B. King, Carl Perkins, and others got their start. Not to mention Beale Street, Stax Records, Sun Records and its world-famous studio, and Graceland. Plus, Memphis is within driving distance of Nashville.

I had one week off between boot camp and the start of my new life in Memphis. I did not want to go home after boot camp because I was so happy with my new life adventure; why go back to the misery for even one week? But I had nowhere else to go. I flew home, dumped my sea bag in my room, hugged my mother, and jetted out of the house without talking to anybody. I spent the week falling back into my old routine of avoiding family members.

MEMPHIS. I TINGLED with excitement as the plane touched down at the airport. I already imagined my life as a musician and could not wait to explore what I considered an American Music Mecca. I enlisted for three years, and by the time I finished my school in Memphis, I would only have a little more than two years to go! But upon boarding the shuttle bus to the Naval base, I was hit with my first big disappointment. Naval Aviation Technical Training Center, Memphis, Tennessee, is not actually based in Memphis proper. It was, in fact, in Millington, Tennessee, about seventeen miles north of Memphis.

The second disappointment came the next day at the base when I found myself working in the galley, the cafeteria that fed the entire airbase 24/7. My new life in Millington meant a month of rotating shifts, twelve hours one day, sixteen hours the next day, twelve hours the next day, and so on. It was mandatory for all trainees to do thirty days in the galley cleaning, mopping, serving, peeling, and cooking until the new class schedule started. To say it sucked was an understatement. Any time off was spent sleeping in World War II barracks with no air conditioning during an incredibly hot, humid summer. A visit to my mecca, Memphis, would have to wait.

But the visit was worth the wait. Memphis, in the summer of 1978, looked as though it hadn't changed since World War II. I did all of the touristy stuff—visited Graceland, Sun Studios, Beale Street—but I also walked around some of the older neighborhoods and visited the rail yards where there were vintage trains. They had churches on just about every corner and on Sundays, when you walked down the street, you could hear incredible performances by gospel choirs. Being from the North, it was hard not to notice that even in 1978 there was still a racial divide, which I imagined was prevalent throughout much of the South. Although you can hear live music during the day at some places, night time is when Beale Street is straight up electrified blues. The live performances carried outside of the clubs and permeated the air.

While in Memphis, I was hell bent on finally being able to buy myself a name brand electric guitar. I wanted a Gibson SG because it was what Frank Zappa played. I walked into one store featuring a huge collection of vintage guitars. I found a custom 1963 Gibson SG. It was beat up with little chips in the finish, white with gold-plated hardware. I fell in love with it instantly. I bought this guitar, and it became my pride and joy. I did not have an amplifier yet, but I bought an instructional book, *Mickey Baker's Jazz Guitar.* I had no idea who Mickey Baker was until years later when I learned he was Mickey of Mickey & Sylvia, the '50s R&B duo who sang the hit single "Love is Strange." Sylvia would later be known as Sylvia Robinson, whose Sugar Hill Records was one of the first pioneering record companies in hip-hop.

At the end of our schooling in Memphis, we were given the opportunity, based on class rank, to select where we would be stationed. I was number three in a class of twenty-four, made up of sailors and marines. The person who was ranked number two got busted for weed and sent to the brig, and the guy who was number one only wanted to go to San Diego, so this left me with a choice of some really exotic places: Hawaii, the Philippines, Japan, the Azores, even Guantanamo Bay, Cuba. But I wanted to be in California.

My brother, Robert, and my sisters, Meg and Ann, all now lived in the Golden State, and, as they were my nice family members, I wanted to be near them. But, just as importantly, I wanted to be a professional musician. Therefore, Los Angeles was the place for me. A pamphlet for a Naval Air Base in Lemoore, California, caught my eye. With its collage of images showing giant redwood trees, mountaintops, and waterfalls, it looked like paradise. But, more importantly to me, it was located in California at almost the halfway point between L.A., 193 miles, and San Francisco, 187 miles.

After a quick stay with my sister, Meg, in L.A., she drove me up to Lemoore to start this next adventure. As we approached, we drove through an area mainly populated by industrial-scale farming tracts. There were no redwoods, waterfalls, mountains, or any of the paradisiacal features depicted in the pamphlet. Instead, there was only brown dirt stretching as far as the horizon, with the occasional little bobbing oil rigs resembling lonely hobby horses grazing in the middle of nowhere. Some were painted to resemble ponies with big eyes and big smiling mouths, as though they were laughing at me for being an idiot. My heart sunk. I had unknowingly committed myself to being stationed in the middle of the desert. I couldn't believe it. I could have gone to Hawaii, but instead I chose this place to be near L.A., where I hoped to further my musical ambition.

After checking into my barracks, I walked around to check out my surroundings, my home for the next three years. The air had a very strange chemical smell to it, which I later realized was insecticide used on the neighboring fields. The base was geographically divided up into two areas. The main base housed administration buildings, living quarters, barracks, galleys, sports fields, Navy housing, a movie theater, stores, and clubs for the enlisted and officers. The operations area—where the hangars, squadrons, and runways were—sat five miles away. I felt lonely and depressed.

I reported to my squadron, VA-122, the next day. VA-122 trained pilots for the Vought A-7 Corsair Light attack jet bomber. This plane, and others like it, were simply airborne weapon platforms for delivering death from above. My job was to load bombs, rockets, and missiles and service the armament systems and aircraft guns. Initially, I was on the graveyard shift, a skeletal crew assigned to work from 11:30 p.m. to 8:30 a.m. I slept during the day; I woke between 8:00 and 9:00 p.m. There was not much time to socialize. Socially, this put me on the back foot when it came to making friends.

In the fall of 1978 I was working the graveyard shift, which was exhausting. Not because of the actual work, but because sleeping during the day was almost impossible. We lived in two-man rooms in buildings resembling dormitories. Most other sailors who worked regular schedules had no regard for people on the graveyard shift, who slept during the day. They would play loud music, yell right outside your window, or often have conversations in the hallway outside your door. About two months after I started this schedule, I was dragging at work. Then someone introduced me to Black Beauties, a prescription amphetamine. I had smoked weed before but had quit when I joined the Navy. My belief at the time was that anything pill related was addictive, so I declined the ominous-looking black capsules at first. But when I started seeing other sailors using them who did not appear to be addicts, I decided to try them. They were cheap and easy to get. I had no inclination of the consequences in the years to come.

I lacked confidence in social situations, and due to my work schedule, I had a tough time making friends. But one day that changed. Sitting alone in my room at the barracks, I was trying to get through the chord progressions for the Chuck Mangione track "Feels So Good." The song was a huge jazz crossover pop hit, and *Guitar Player* magazine published the guitar solo. I was not a huge fan of the song, but I just wanted to learn the underlying chord changes. Suddenly, somebody knocked on my door. It was an African-American guy from down the hall,

Audi Phipps. I had seen Audi around; he was an aviation electrician mate, but I had never talked to him.

Audi, as it turned out, played guitar and keyboards. A Chicago native, he was an aspiring R&B songwriter. He heard me trying to play this song and showed me easier ways to play some of the harder chords. This was the first of many mentoring sessions with Audi, who taught me R&B music and about the importance of songwriting. Audi showed me how songs were structured and what made songs work. He was very generous with his time given I was a novice.

Audi's lessons gave me an appreciation for songwriting and an everlasting respect and admiration for people who had the God-given ability to write songs. I realized that popular music did not require you to be a virtuoso musician but rather to have the ability to tell stories through music. It made me look at all the artists I had been listening to over the years with a whole new appreciation. Because Audi's forte was R&B, everything he taught me was from an R&B perspective, but he was always keen to point out it was applicable to rock, pop, and country. This is where my love affair with R&B music began. Audi turned me on to artists like the Ohio Players, Brass Construction, Marvin Gaye, Bill Withers, Sly & the Family Stone, the Temptations, and others.

Because I was from Philadelphia, Audi talked about what Philadelphia meant to black music and the Philadelphia International Records Legacy (PIR). Philadelphia had always been a mainstay city for R&B and jazz, which should not be surprising given its proximity to New York. But what really defined Philadelphia in the eyes of the music industry was PIR. As a teen, I was aware of Philly International and its owners, Kenny Gamble and Leon Huff, who were writers and producers. I had read an article about them in *Philadelphia Magazine*. I certainly knew of PIR's artists Teddy Pendergrass, Patti LaBelle, the O'Jays, the Intruders, and Billy Paul, mostly because I used to watch *Soul Train* with Terry Akins at his house, but it was not until I had met Audi that I realized how important this label's contribution was to black music. At the time, I could have never imagined I would years later be doing deals with Kenny Gamble.

I started working the day shift at the squadron, which was when operations were at their peak. It was a dangerous, fast-paced environment. Like with my childhood, music became my constant and my therapy. When not at the squadron, I played music every chance I got. Audi introduced me to other musicians who soon became my friends. I felt like part of this social microcosm of sailors who happened to be musicians, or as I saw it, musicians who happened to be sailors. Some of them were so musically accomplished I could not understand why they joined the service. I thought if I was that good, I would be out trying to make it as a pro. I was a bit of a hack; even worse, I was a hack who could not see the limitations of my own abilities.

In the spring of 1979, I started a band with some other sailors who tolerated my musical shortcomings as a diversion from the routine of military life. Despite my inabilities, I still wanted to make it as a professional musician. The manager of the enlisted men's club let me use a vacant building on the property, which had once housed a liquor store, as a practice space. It had its own raised area, like a stage, as well as its own parking area and was secluded from the main structure.

Our drummer, fellow squadron mate Bobby Caliguri, was from Huntington Beach, California. We called him Surfin' Bob because he grew up in a family of surfers. We had another guitar player named Pete Cavanaugh. We also had a violinist in our band named Orlando Moss. His father, Orlando Moss, Sr., was a famous African-American opera vocal instructor who wrote books about opera. Orlando was primarily a classically trained violinist, but he loved jazz. He taught me to read music. Our repertoire was limited to only things I could play. We kept changing bass players for different reasons. We played a cover of Jean-Luc Ponty's "Imaginary Voyage Part IV," mainly because it had only four chords and had a very cool spacey intro. And we played a somewhat passable version of Weather Report's "Birdland." We soon had about forty-five minutes of music we could stretch to an hour and a half by just jamming out.

In summer of 1979, we played our first gig at the Naval Air Station Lemoore Annual Air Show, a public event featuring a vintage aircraft display, stunt fliers, and other attractions. The main event was the U.S. Navy flight demonstration team, the Blue Angels. The Blue Angels were the Cirque du Soleil of military aviation, flying their bright blue A-4 Skyhawks in precision formation doing hair-raising stunts. The Blue Angels were handpicked from the Navy's very best pilots. Wearing our dress white uniforms, my band played on the back of a flatbed ground support vehicle set up on the tarmac in front of the parked Blue Angels A-4s. There was no PA system. We were told to play for fifteen minutes. We played an extended version of a Jean-Luc Ponty song and an extended instrumental version of a Flora Purim song. Both had long, spacey intros and gave Orlando wide-open room to solo. The crowd gave us enthusiastic applause, which I suspected was more out of patriotic reverence rather than appreciation of our musical offering.

After that first gig, we were offered a show with the U.S. Navy Jazz Band at a Navy base in San Francisco called Treasure Island. They gave us a passenger van, and the admiral's office gave us request slips authorizing us for what they called "collateral duty," meaning we could miss work for the show. I was happier than I'd ever been before. A band I had started was being subsidized by the Navy to do a show in San Francisco. We were given per diem money and gas money for the van since this was considered a deployment. I realized I could do anything involving music as long as I had the right people around me.

We drove 190 miles up I-5 on Friday to San Francisco and checked into the Treasure Island Naval Base. They gave us rooms in the transient barracks, and we were to report the next day to the theatre for sound check. That night, we explored San Francisco. Saturday afternoon, we went over to the theatre. There were people setting up to rehearse while a guy sat at a piano singing, or rather whispering, "Colour my World" by Chicago, completely off key. We were a little confused.

As it turns out, we were not there to perform a typical gig. Unbeknownst to us, we were participating in a talent show, and the U.S. Navy Jazz Band was not performing but rather accompanying contestants for the show. This was completely deflating. We were not told we were being sent to a talent show. The admiral's office had sent us to compete in this event to represent Naval Air Station Lemoore. The event coordinator told us we would perform just one song. Trying to make the best of it, we played a shortened version of the Jean-Luc Ponty song. We lost, of course. Not that we cared.

The next morning, the smell of weed from the room next to me in the barracks wafted into the hallway. While I'd partaken in the drug during junior high and high school, I had left it alone in the service. Still, I knew what I was smelling, and it was coming from the room of two of my band mates. I was lying in my bed when I heard loud banging in the hallway. I opened my door to see four Naval Investigative Service guys in black uniforms banging on the door with a nightstick. My band mates were taken in and written up. This was bad.

We had to get the van back to base for the NAS Lemoore flag football team, who was scheduled to use it to go down to San Diego for a game, but this debacle caused us to leave San Francisco five hours late. When we pulled into the base and parked the van, a Chief Petty Officer walked up and asked very loudly if we cleaned all of the "Paca Lolo" out of it. He was talking about the weed. This was bad. The two band members ended up going to "XOI" (executive officer's interrogation), which is the first phase of the military justice system. The two band members were sentenced to correctional custody, and I had to hear shit from disgruntled flag football team members, who had to carpool down to San Diego because we did not get the van back in time.

The band continued to do small gigs throughout my remaining two-plus years at Lemoore, mainly entertaining drunken sailors and marines who complained about the lack of Tom Petty and Van Halen in our repertoire. Truth be told, I did not even know how to play the most basic of rock songs. As a kid, I had this misguided idea in my head that I could maybe become a jazz player. Therefore, after the Navy I wanted to move to L.A., which had a big jazz scene.

A phone call with my childhood friend, Jeff Coulter, changed it all. Jeff and I had not talked since I joined the Navy, so I called him to catch up and talk about family, the Navy, and, of course, music. Like me, Jeff was also actively playing music. He'd expanded his skills beyond the drums and was now into electronic music. We bonded over our new equipment: me with my Deagan Electravibes (a set of vibraphones set up in a case with attachable legs so you can carry them), effects pedals, and my echoplex tape echo unit, and he with his synthesizers and programmable sequencers. We discussed the electronic-based music coming from Europe—groups like Gong, Cluster, Robert Fripp, Brian Eno, Tangerine Dream, and others, and in particular our mutual love of the German electronic group Kraftwerk.

By the time we ended the call, I made a decision that, although I did not know it at that time, would change the course of my life. I told Jeff I would move back to Philadelphia to start a band with him.

Before I left the West Coast, my brother, Bob, threw a surprise going away party for me in L.A. and had all my friends from Lemoore come down. In January 1981, the morning after my last day of active duty, I walked to the main gates of the airbase. While I carried my duffel bag and two electric guitar cases, I was filled with excitement at the anticipation of doing music full-time. I was about forty feet away from the gates when I saw the shuttle bus to the Fresno airport about to depart. I broke into a jog, but, just as I was about to set foot off of government property, the marines who manned the gatehouse and directed traffic yelled at me to stop. They halted traffic and blew their whistles. It was time for morning colors, the raising of the flag. Everyone on base had to stop to face the flag as it was raised, including me, a mere five steps away from the gates. As the flag was raised up the pole, the shuttle van on the other side of the chain link fence pulled away.

Luckily, I was hours early, so I did not mind waiting for the next shuttle. I flew back to Philly, and my father picked me up at the airport. All of my equipment (except my guitars) was shipped back and due to arrive in a few days. My older brothers had moved out of the house, leaving just my three younger siblings living at home. After I got home and dumped my stuff at my house, I borrowed my brother Karl's motorcycle and rode over to Jeff's.

In Jeff's bedroom wall-to-wall keyboards sat where his drums once sat. He had a vast record collection of music from artists all over the world, the majority which he bought as imports from Plastic Fantastic in Ardmore, an independent record store specializing in imports or Third Street Jazz in Philly, probably one of the best record stores in the city.

It was so great to see Jeff, and it was particularly exciting that he was also playing music, especially the progressive electronic stuff. This was 1981 and digital sampling was yet to become a staple of music production. Up until then, drum loops and the actual manipulation of a vinyl record by a DJ was still in its infancy. To be able to sample even a second of music and then be able to play it back at will required technology far beyond what was available to musicians at that time.

At the time, Kraftwerk were probably the most commercially successful artists in the electronic music genre next to Walter (later Wendy) Carlos. Kraftwerk had been part of the electronic music movement, which started in Germany in the '60s. Jeff and I had been huge fans of Kraftwerk since school. Two of their compositions, "Numbers" and "Trans-Europe Express," would become break-dance anthems, and Kraftwerk would musically influence the entire hip-hop genre more than anybody else. It was not until their fourth album, *Autobahn*, featuring the twenty-three-minute title track of the same name, played on AM pop radio that their name became synonymous with electronic music.

The electronic music movement had evolved from the roots of Europe's progressive art rock scene but was different because German bands tended to use simplistic regimented rhythms. *Autobahn* was not completely an electronic album. It featured flute and guitar, as well. The piece was inspired by Germany's world-famous Autobahn motorway, which connects every major German city with no speed limit.

Jeff also had albums by artists who were considered obscure in the United States but were commercially viable in Europe. I loved to play this type of music because of the artistic freedom it offered, and it did not require musical virtuosity on my part. Jeff was an accomplished drummer and was very skilled at programming interlocking melodies fired by an analog sequencer with complex rhythmic structures. The sequences were dark and rhythmically aggressive. This gave me a musical palette to create melodic harmonies on guitar through tape loops and other effects. We created musical landscapes of such complexity that we did not sound like just two people. We played almost every night, amassing material. We called ourselves Tangent.

Robert Fripp, the guitarist and founder of the pioneering progressive rock group King Crimson, had been experimenting with tape loops and had created a system called "Frippertronics." It was really quite simple but genius: He used two Revox tape decks looped together with one continuous length of tape. It gave him the ability to play a note, or sequence of notes, which played back on tape while he then played overlapping harmonies. It went on continuously as the original lines faded while the new lines evolved melodically. It sounded like an orchestral montage. Now, to be fair, Les Paul had done that in the '50s, but in a different way for a completely different genre of music.

It took Jeff and me no time to set up our own version of a tape loop system, which I used frequently. What really brought things together was our purchase of a Roland TR-808 Rhythm

Composer programmable drum machine. This was the first drum machine ever that was not just a box of preprogrammed factory rhythms; it was revolutionary in that you could build actual drum programs. The TR-808 later became massively influential in the world of hip-hop, but we had no idea at that time. In the commercial musical instrument market, the 808 was considered a failure, and it was only available for three years. However, its individual instrument sounds became iconic, particularly the cowbell, wood block, hand claps, and kick drum, which had a unique feature allowing the user to set the rate of decay. Because most rap artists did not have sufficient outboard gear to separate or manipulate the 808 kick drum, they would turn up the decay to give it more bottom, creating a distinctive sound that became synonymous with eighties hip-hop. We used the 808 giving each instrument its own channel in the mixing board so that, when we performed, the drums gave us a sonic punch similar to Kraftwerk's sound.

WXPN, the University of Pennsylvania's public radio station, was considered to be one of the most influential college radio stations in the country, particularly in the triple A radio genre (Adult Album Alternative). The station played a large variety of cutting-edge music in every format, including rock, folk, blues, Americana, and world music. It also played and supported electronic music in a big way. WXPN broadcast two nightly shows, *Diaspar* and *Star's End*. Both shows featured electronic music. The shows were programmed and hosted by John Diliberto, Gino Wong, Kim Haas, Michele Polizi, and others. It was incredible the station not only broadcast electronic music, it also hosted live on-air performances and sponsored shows at different venues.

Jeff and I eventually made a tape for WXPN, which we dropped off at the station for John Diliberto. It was as simple as driving down to Fortieth and Spruce Street in West Phila-delphia and giving a tape to whomever had answered the door. It was not long until we heard one of our compositions played on *Star's End*. We took a break from recording one night to listen to the show, not really expecting to hear our music, but at the beginning of the broadcast John Diliberto announced to listeners he would be playing music from a new group. I was twenty years old, and I had been out of the Navy for less than two months, and I had music being played on a Philadelphia radio station. Not only did they play it, they actually talked about it, mentioning our names!

In Philadelphia at the time, there were less than a handful of local artists doing this kind of music. Others in our genre included Paul Woznicki (known as "Woz"), the Night Crawlers (three guys who each had an array of keyboards), and the Ghostwriters (two guys named Charles Cohen and Jeff Cain). I think WXPN was interested in us because, right after the debut, they asked us to perform at a picnic they had every year outside the station at the intersection of Forty-Second and Spruce in West Philly.

We packed everything into my 1970 Chevy Caprice Estate station wagon and drove down to West Philadelphia. The pic-nic featured artists representing every format of music played on WXPN. It was our first live performance, and although it was a mixed crowd, it went over fairly well. This led to a succes-sion of shows promoted by WXPN. We did live broadcast per-formances from their studio at Forty-Second and Spruce, as well as shows at St. Mary's, a venue on the Penn campus that was formerly a church. We did other gigs at places like the Painted Bride Art Center in Old City and other small venues.

Around this time, I got a job as a cook at a restaurant chain called H.A. Winston & Co., at their Paoli location. I worked at

Winstons during the day and played music with Jeff at night, and the WXPN performances led to more opportunities. We got a gig at a place called the East Side Club. The East Side Club was one of the many venues that made up Philly's burgeoning live music scene. Other venues included the London Victory Club, the Hot Club, Stephen Starr's Ripley Music Hall, Grendel's Lair, the Khyber Pass, and Dobb's on South Street.

During one performance at the East Side Club, we switched it up and performed the entire album version of Kraftwerk's "Autobahn." It was this performance that set off a chain of key events in my musical career. Debbie Kaminski, a filmmaker, had watched our set and afterward offered to collaborate with us on some projects. Debbie was affiliated with a collective of artists and musicians who were all part of the post-punk music and art scene. I was invited to one of their parties where I met a guy named Danny Mason. Danny was from Boston and had come to Villanova to join the seminary, but that did not work out. He was the singer for a band called Rhythm of Lines (ROL), who took its name from a Mondrian painting and was considered to be one of the best up-and-coming local bands in Philly. The band had been doing shows mainly opening up for established bands, like the Vels, the Stick Men, and the Bunnydrums. ROL was very much influenced by the Talking Heads, especially with their use of syncopated funk rhythms.

Danny was very interested in Jeff and me joining his band. He likened the idea to "the Army getting an Air Force."

The combined band was made up of Jeff and me, as well as Danny playing guitar and vocals, Jay McClenegan, a classically trained bassist, and Greg "Doc" DeSabatino on drums. At first, it was very cool. Combining the programmed 808 with the live drums, we came up with some really intricate, infectious grooves. Danny had this very deep voice, sort of like an Ian

Curtis/Joy Division vibe. The band rehearsed in an apartment located on the second floor above a bar. We did a ton of gigs starting out as openers for more established groups, but then we started to headline our own shows, some at the East Side Club. We also cut some songs at a studio on Chestnut Street.

Other bands were starting to get noticed. The Vels had secured a record deal with PolyGram. It was about songs, and the Vels had made it work with simple hooks. And Pretty Poison, who we had also played with a bunch of times, got a deal on Atlantic. They had recorded a song called "Catch Me (I'm Falling)." The track (mixed by Joe Nicolo) had incorporated electronic elements similar to ours, including the TR-808 firing analog sequences. This was a very hot sound made popular by artists like Shannon, whose song "Let the Music Play" on Emergency Records was a dance floor anthem. I would constantly point to artists like Depeche Mode, Information Society, and New Order who were leading this genre. The Vels and Pretty Poison had started in this post-punk underground scene, and they eventually evolved to creating a repertoire that was played on the radio. It seemed like the right direction to go in, but Danny, Jay, and Greg did not want to hear it. They wanted the music we were doing to be more obscure. I did not understand it, nor did I need to be in a band to create "obscure" music. I could do that all day long with Jeff doing electronic music for our WXPN audience. I made my feelings known at a rehearsal one day, mentioning the Vels' success at having more commercial songs, and my comments were not received very well. After that, rehearsals started to become a drag. I wanted to get a record deal. Plain and simple. Jeff and I left the band.

Soon after, Debbie Kaminski introduced me to a friend of hers from film school, Rich Murray. Rich was a filmmaker who, along with Debbie, had graduated from Temple University's Radio, Television, and Film program. He was doing some commercial work shooting industrial videos. Rich had done a music video for a local artist, Alan Mann. Alan's song was called "Christmas on the Block," and Rich's video became the first independent music video ever shown on MTV. Rich and I talked about our mutual interests and soon became friends. Rich lived in a large house with other roommates, people who he knew from the film production business, on Hazel Avenue in West Philadelphia. There were people moving out, and Rich needed new roommates to cover the rent. It seemed like the perfect opportunity to move into Philly where we could set up a studio. Jeff liked the idea, as well. We moved into that huge house in a predominately African-American neighborhood not far from the University of Pennsylvania campus.

We were all guys in our early twenties trying to get our shit together to get established in life. Rich, Jeff, and I were trying to establish careers in the entertainment arts. Jeff and I started to amass a huge collection of twelve-inch dance records, and we put together tracks in a studio we created in one of the bedrooms. We listened to all sorts of music that came from New York in the early eighties—predominately dance music being released on the multitude of independent labels. We set our sights on doing our own commercial production.

Not long after we moved in, Jeff and I were part of an event at the Painted Bride Art Center, where artists doing experimental music and performance art came together. After our set, I noticed a beautiful girl with long blonde hair putting away a saxophone in a case. I got back to packing up our gear when somebody tapped me on the shoulder. I turned around, and it was her. She thought our set was really cool, and she asked if we could jam sometime. Her name was Robin Carter but was also known as "Astro Girl" due to her affinity for anything related to space travel. (She later went on to earn a degree in astrophysics and work for NASA.)

Robin lived in a West Philly rental on Spring Garden Street. Her landlord, Jack Wright, was a locally renowned avant-garde jazz saxophonist. He performed with a group called Spring Garden Music, which musically took its cues from artists like Ornette Coleman and Sun Ra. I was familiar with Spring Garden Music as they played around quite often, and I had heard them on Temple University's WRTI jazz program. Robin's association with that group made her very attractive to me—beautiful, talented, and a musician who was into cool music. Robin was really into R&B, especially Teena Marie. Robin had a spectacular singing voice, and I thought she would be the perfect addition to our dance music production. She started singing over tracks that Jeff and I wrote.

Robin had a boyfriend, a bass player, who, it seemed, was in and out of her life. While I had a thing for her, I kept it to myself; until one day while we were alone in the studio, she initiated sex. It was totally unexpected. I admittedly had not much experience with women. The relationship never came to fruition because Robin was still in love with the other guy.

IN THE SUMMER of 1983, Rich was hired to direct videos for a newly established record label in Philadelphia called Philly World. Philly World, for all intents and purposes, was sort of a knock-off of Kenny Gamble and Leon Huff's Philadelphia International Records (PIR). PIR recorded all of their records at Sigma Sound Studios while Philly World recorded at Alpha International Studios, which was their base of operations. Philly World's roster consisted of artists who were formerly on

PIR during its heyday. One of these artists was Harold Melvin and the Blue Notes. Rich was working on a video for them, and he got me the gig as a caterer, given my experience in my day job as a cook at a local restaurant. As a result, I would often myself be hired as the caterer on the sets of these shoots while Rich filmed.

It was on one of those video shoots I met a Philly World producer named Donald Robinson. I told Donald about what I was doing with Jeff and Robin, and I invited him to the house to check us out. After calling him a million times, he finally came over. Donald was very cool, and I was actually amazed he came over. As a novice in the business, I was thrilled to have the opportunity to engage with a bona fide producer who had songs on the radio. He listened to us, and I think he got it on some level. He understood what type of sound we were going for. But after listening to a number of our tracks, he told us we needed better songs—and that we should call him when we had them. I was disappointed, but I thought back to when I was hanging out with Audi Phipps and everything he had taught me. Songwriting is a craft, and we just needed to get better at it. It would only be a matter of time.

By this time, Jeff and I had become very proficient at programming the TR-808. What started for us as a component for the writing and production of electronic music soon became a staple in dance music. Robin got us a gig at the Gallery Mall on Market Street in Center City. This was a little different from our previous gigs. First off, it's a mall. Who played a gig in a shopping mall? The Gallery Mall was also popular among African-American shoppers—a completely different audience than we were used to.

During our set, most people watched for a few minutes and then walked away. But a young group of African-American kids were hanging out talking intensely among themselves while they watched us. At the end of our set they walked over to us. They introduced themselves as a rap group and asked if we could do some beats for them. Jeff and I agreed immediately.

Hip-hop was exciting; for me, there was nothing not to love about it. It was storytelling over electronic drum programs and loops. It had the storytelling element of R&B and the syncopated percussion of electronic music. We exchanged phone numbers with the group, packed our gear, and went home.

That night, I got a call from one of the kids from the mall. His name was Clinton Shirley, and he went by the name Kidd Fresh. He came over with his crew the next Sunday night. At this time, hip-hop was still in its embryonic stage and, production-wise, pretty simple. We did a couple of solid tracks, doing some drum programs for them and recording tracks on our Teac 4 track. Once everything was complete, we had just the one question: What do we do with it?

CHAPTER THREE

1618 N. BROAD STREET

Frank Virtue's recording studio was on the second floor above a check cashing establishment in North Philly at the intersection of Broad Street and Columbia. I rang the buzzer on a steel security door and announced myself through the security intercom. The door buzzed, and I climbed the steps to the second floor. There was a little reception room where the walls were adorned with framed gold 45 rpm records. The room was dark except for a single window in the control room, accentuated by some '60s-era mood lighting fixtures on the ceilings. I read off the titles of the framed gold 45s: "Guitar Boogie Shuffle," "The Horse," "The Return of the Horse"—all by the Virtues—"Hey There Lonely Girl" by Eddie Holman, and some others. I could not help but notice the bullet trap against the wall. I recognized it from when I had small arms training in the service. It was a steel contraption designed for firing a gun into. It seemed out of place in a recording studio.

Frank came out of the control room and introduced himself, asking what I had for him. I'd scored a meeting with Frank after lying about a connection to producer Donald Robinson. I implied that we were more involved with Donald than just the one-time meeting we'd had with him. We went into the control room, which was just big enough for about four people. While Frank put the cassette into a rack-mounted cassette player, I looked at him more closely. Frank had a very unique look with a very prominent hairpiece—sort of like a fifties pompadour, jet black with prominent sideburns, like an aging Elvis impersonator with a mustache. He looked to be in his mid- to late sixties. He wore a long-sleeve collared shirt with a pullover vest, a feeble attempt to cover the massive hand cannon he carried. It was impossible to miss. There were stories about Frank and how he was affiliated with the mob, which I thought was a little ridiculous, but I could see how the gun caused tongues to wag. In truth, Frank was a music business old-timer with a studio in a not-so-great part of town.

Frank had a colorful music career. In his youth, he studied classical music and played violin in the Philadelphia Orchestra. He then took up guitar and upright bass. He joined the Navy in WWII as a bandleader for the U.S. Navy Dance Band. After his discharge, he led a big band of his own. When the era of the big band came to an end, he formed a trio called the Virtues to capitalize on the rock and roll phenomenon ignited by groups like Bill Haley's Comets. He did shows backing up artists such as Patti Page. In the '50s, he released a number of singles under the Virtues moniker with the biggest single, "Guitar Boogie Shuffle," going to number five on the *Billboard* charts. He eventually disbanded the group to go into record engineering and production. Virtue Recording became the go-to studio in Philadelphia for labels like Cameo Parkway and Philadelphia International before the days of Sigma Sound. Frank flew airplanes and had a notable aptitude for electronics. He held patents for pioneering innovations he created that were used in the record mastering process. He also mastered the first singles by the Beatles for their American releases on the Swan and Decca labels.

Frank listened to the Kidd Fresh tracks and definitely wanted to record them. I played him a song Robin, Jeff, and I had done called "Don't Throw Back My Love." Frank listened, but he was not sure about the song.

Frank's business associate, Vince DeRosa, owned a record-pressing plant in New Jersey called Sound Makers. Vince pressed the vinyl for all of the major independent labels out of New York. He was doing a booming business in hip-hop, pressing records for Def Jam, Next Plateau, Sleeping Bag, Tommy Boy, and others. Frank and Vince had decided they wanted some hip-hop records of their own to put out.

So my arrival this day with the hip-hop project in hand was very fortuitous.

But here was the trade-off: In exchange for Frank allowing me to bring in projects to record, I would help him record gospel choirs for local congregations. Frank had a nice business recording local gospel choirs. They would hire Frank to record, master, and press up the records, which they then sold to their respective church members to raise money. I often acted as Frank's assistant, moving microphones and soundproof baffles. It was incredible to hear the gospel singers perform with such passion and emotion, and to do it almost effortlessly. I would forever look at these singers as a musical barometer whenever I listened to aspiring singers later on in my career.

During the fall of 1983, I was in the studio just about every night and on weekends, too. Jeff, Robin, and I signed a recording contract with Frank. It was a one-and-a-half page mimeographed contract. In the space for the artist royalties, it read "5 cent" per record. I was sophisticated enough to know the difference between "cent" and "percentage," but truth be told, I did not care. I had a contract.

Frank mentioned something about recording agreements in a conversation early on in our relationship that I carried with me throughout my career: "It does not matter what the initial recording agreement says because, if the record blows up and becomes successful, then the artist can dictate terms going forward more advantageous than even the most generous first-time agreement." Later in my career, I found it amusing how a new artist's lawyers and managers acted tough during negotiations on their client's agreement. I would tell them repeatedly that I had never seen an artist whose first record goes gold *not* come back and restructure the entire deal, but the lawyers and managers needed to justify their percentage by putting on a show of trying to beat me up on a new artist deal.

At Frank's studio, Jeff, Robin, and I recorded the track "Don't Throw Back My Love" under the name the Ultronics. Admittedly, it was not much more than us trying to imitate some of the hit dance records coming out of New York. It featured heavy use of sequenced bass lines and the TR-808 drum machine with Robin's pseudo Teena Marie vocal performance. Later, Frank and I played it for Vince in the control room. I was hoping Vince would want to press it up and distribute it through his independent distribution. Vince was about Frank's age, but short and gruff, and he wore wide frame glasses with thick lenses. And he always dressed like he worked in a garage. But do not let the attire fool you. Beyond the fact he was a millionaire many times over, he was referred to in the independent record business as "The Godfather of Vinyl."

Vince looked up at the rack-mounted reel-to-reel, squinting, as he took in our song. I watched him for his reaction. He shut it off mid-song, turned to me, and said, "You did this? It sucks!" I was deflated.

Next, Vince listened to the Kidd Fresh demos. Frank and Vince talked in the control room with the door shut. Now this could be something. I sat in the studio live room, contemplating the failure of my own project but hopeful that the Kidd Fresh record would be released.

As Vince left the room, he walked up to me and took a roll of bills out of his pocket. He peeled off five one hundred dollar bills, handed them to me, and left. It's almost twice what I made in a week after taxes at Downey's in my day job as a cook, and it was, at the time, the single largest sum of money I had ever made in music.

In truth, I did not think about money very often in those early days, other than the fact that I did not have any. I wanted to be in the music business, and it was not money that motivated me. But there, with a fresh wad of cash in my hands, I was determined to make it as a producer, and the Kidd Fresh record would be my start.

After it was all said and done, Frank and Vince pressed up the Kidd Fresh record and had some guy in one of the pressing plant pick-up trucks drive Clinton around to radio and club promo dates.

But nothing happened. The record did not spark anybody's attention. I would spend the next year doing various projects at Frank's. We made a number of "sound-a-like" records. This was a popular business practice in the '50s and '60s. A company would have musicians and singers record already existing hit songs and release them as a themed compilation. Frank thought this would be great to do with hit rap songs, due to how easily they could be replicated in the studio. They were kind of hokey with titles like *Rap Explosion Vol 1* and so forth.

In early 1984, I showed up to the studio, and Frank was mastering a record from a cassette for a label called Pop Art Records in Philly. Frank, aside from being a recording engineer and producer, also had a mastering business where he would cut the actual vinyl masters to be used in the record pressing process. The mastering process is what happens after a record is finished and mixed in a studio. After a song gets recorded, it needs to be "mastered" so it can be reproduced with the intended audio equalization for manufacturing, radio broadcast, or any other scenario. Typically, a record is mastered from the finished studio master tape.

Mastering is a specialty that Frank had been doing for years. That day, he was mastering the vinyl disc that would be used to create the stampers for the pressing machines. The vinyl cut from the lathe is dipped into a bath charged with electricity, which causes metal particles to form an opposite disc, like a photo negative. This is called a "mother." The mother is then used to create the stampers, which are attached to the pressing machine that presses the liquid vinyl composite into a vinyl record. The cutting lathe used to create the original vinyl master looks like a massive sewing machine. Frank was sitting at the lathe cutting the vinyl master, telling me the studio master tape was actually a cassette of a song that was a hit record in New York City called "Roxanne's Revenge" by a rapper named Roxanne Shante. It was on Pop Art

Records, a Philadelphia record label run by two brothers, Lawrence and Dana Goodman.

The song was getting massive airplay in New York on WBLS, which was one of the most influential radio stations in the country. The song was an "answer record" to UTFO's "Roxanne, Roxanne." In the early days of hip-hop, it was popular for artists to make "answer records" where the song would be a response to an already popular song on the radio. I had an idea. I got the phone number for Pop Art and called the number and talked to Lawrence Goodman. I introduced myself and told Lawrence I had a film production company and we could do a video for "Roxanne's Revenge."

My roommate, Rich Murray, thought that could be a great platform to start a music video production company. We went over to Lawrence's house to talk about a video. We agreed to a price—two thousand dollars—which was a far cry from the eventual budgets of millions I would spend on music videos in the years to come. Even in the early days of music video production, two thousand was a fraction of the production value Rich put on the screen. Rich pulled out all the stops and begged, borrowed, and stole, facilitating his relationships with everybody he knew in the Philadelphia film production community.

We filmed the opening sequence of the video at our house on Hazel Avenue in West Philly. Roxanne Shante smashed records against the front of the house while lip synching the opening lines to the song: "Why ya have to make a record 'bout me?" The video was inventive and funny, following the storyline of the song about how she got discovered. It featured some awesome dance sequences. We cast Fat Larry, a drummer in a band that was signed to Fantasy Records called Fat Larry's Band, as a cop who was there to answer to a disturbance. The video also featured Mr. Magic, an on-air personality from WBLS, as well as song producer Marley Marl, who was also a mix show DJ on WBLS. Clinton "Kidd Fresh" Shirley was cast as a member of the fake UTFO. The filming was at multiple locations and went long into the night. There were hundreds of onlookers on Hazel Ave. The neighbors across the street called our landlord, who showed up in the middle of filming and was not happy.

In the morning, I came down to the living room to find Mr. Magic and Marley Marl lying on couches under blankets eating cereal and watching cartoons. These were some of the most influential guys in hip-hop at the time, and they were in my living room watching TV. It was surreal.

The video exceeded expectations. It got played on MTV, BET, and MusicBox. Now we had an established business template on how to go to other independent labels in New York to pitch our music video production services. Our idea was to use the Roxanne Shante video as an example of how affordable a video could be. I went through our collection of twelve-inch hip-hop and dance records and compiled a list of labels with addresses and phone numbers. I called them to set up appointments and found that, although receptive, most of these companies did not even have television monitors to watch videos because videos at the time were a promotional luxury only the major labels could facilitate. The cost of making a video for an indie record label was often more than the cost to record a song, press it up, and distribute it. Rich and I went to New York one day carrying a television set around to the offices of all of these independent labels. What surprised me was that, although some of these companies had successful records, their offices were very unassuming and were predominately staffed by just a few people. Profile Records, run by Cory Robbins and

Steve Plotnicki and home to Run-DMC, consisted of a two-room office in midtown on Broadway, but without a TV. After we watched the Roxanne video on our traveling television set, Cory and Steve kept us there for another hour so they could watch a stack of videos they had but had no way to look at them.

While the scouting trip to New York wasn't successful, it gave me an idea of what an independent label was truly all about. By spring of 1984, I decided that, to be successful in this business, I needed to find a job with a record label. I'd hit a low point in my life both personally and professionally, and Robin finally made it clear there was no future for me as her boyfriend. I watched her date other guys, but the straw that broke the camel's back was when she ditched me at a New Year's Eve party to leave with her ex-boyfriend. My tenure with Frank Virtue had pretty much run its course. It was a studio-based production operation but far from being a record company. I had spent a year schlepping back and forth from Frank's and helped Rich with the videos, but I was still working as a cook during the day and making so little money I could barely make rent. I was frustrated; I put things in motion, but I could not crack the code. I wanted to make it in the music business, but nothing came to fruition. Up until now, I seemed to meet the right people, but I could not parlay these connections into something bigger.

One afternoon, while looking through the *Philadelphia Weekly* job listings, an ad jumped off the page at me: Record company looking for help. I called the number and talked with a guy named Ted Wing. I gave Ted a rundown on what I had done with Frank and my own production background. Ted told me his company was called Nicetown Records. It was essentially an independent record company doing R&B. We set up a time for me to come over the next day.

The next morning, I suited up. I decided to walk to the place, located at Fifty-Second and Parkside in West Philly. I walked farther west from Forty-Eighth Street, passed blocks of row houses on every block, and as I turned right to walk up Fifty-Second Street, I could not help but notice I was the only white person in the entire area, and I was getting more than a few occasional double glances. A group of teenagers walked past me commenting, "Talk about being in the wrong neighborhood," followed by raucous laughter. I finally arrived at the address near Fifty-Second and Parkside.

I looked down at the address written on my paper and confirmed this was the spot. The building in front of me was an old, turn-of-the-century three-story featuring a large, steel security door; windows covered with thick, metal screens; and a big sign outside: Tender Care Day Care Center. Maybe I had the wrong address? I finally decided to knock on the door. I knocked a number of times until a teenage girl yelled from behind the window for me to go around to the side door, another big, steel security door. I hit the buzzer and waited.

Finally, after almost ten minutes, an elderly lady opened the door about four inches and said in the most uninviting tone possible, "What do you want?"

"I may have the wrong address," I apologized, "but I'm here for an interview with Ted Wing."

"That's my son, wait!" she said and slammed the door in my face.

I stood outside for another ten minutes, thinking maybe this was just where Ted wanted to meet, that possibly the record company was located somewhere else. When the elderly lady opened the door again, I walked in to a cacophony of screaming toddlers and babies being cared for by a group of tired-looking, dispassionate teenage girls. The place smelled like poop and urine. Ted's mother directed me to a wall lined with chairs about a foot high, designed for little kids. She barked at me to sit down and wait for Ted. I sat on one of these little chairs for twenty minutes waiting for Ted, thinking maybe this would not be the dream job I thought it was. Finally, the side door from the outside opened and Ted arrived, unapologetically late.

Ted walked me to the back of the daycare center into a suite of offices draped in carpet, wood paneling, and soft lighting. A former prison guard at Graterford Prison, Ted wanted to get into the record business. During our interview, Ted explained his vision for Nicetown Records and how he was going to make Nicetown a premier independent R&B label. He had recently signed Bunny Sigler, a celebrated artist/writer on Philadelphia International Records in its heyday. Ted also had a taped performance of Bill Cosby performing standup live at Graterford Prison. In Bill Cosby's arrangement with the prison administration, he allowed the prison to retain the rights to the tapes with any derived proceeds going to the prisoners' activity program. Ted was the director of that program, and, as a result, he ended up with the tapes. Ted showed me the "artwork" for the forthcoming *Bill Cosby live at Graterford Prison* album release on Nicetown Records. Since Ted did not have rights for photo images of Bill Cosby, he had a rendering done that was straight-up hideous, a black-and-orange image of Bill Cosby with an elongated head looking like an alien. It wasn't going to sell, I thought as Ted proudly showed off the art.

Ted offered me $120 a week. He took me up to my "office" on the third floor of this building—a dilapidated room with no heating or air conditioning, walls of crumbling plaster, and dirty windows that were nailed shut. I had a desk with a phone and a chair.

In those early days, Ted showed me the ropes. He gave me a *Billboard* magazine and explained the black album chart. In order to get your record positioned on the chart, a select panel of music retailers across the country reported your title selling X amount of units at their location that week. This information was compiled every week by *Billboard* via phone and was used to determine the chart positioning of that particular title. At the time, there were about 120 retail stores reporting in to the black album sales chart.

The chart, like all other sales and airplay charts prior to the advent of SoundScan and BDS (Nielsen Broadcast Data Systems), with some finesse, could be manipulated by the record labels. It was a simple process: You gave the retailer free product that they could sell without paying the distributor, and since it was profitable, they were motivated to encourage customers to buy it, and they reported the sales to *Billboard*. The sales were tallied by the *Billboard* staff, and, as a result, the titles were awarded a position on the chart. The thousands of other retailers across the country would see the title debut on the chart and order it from the distributor, and so on. This explanation is very simplistic and is obviously lacking description and details regarding the variables and nuances, but you get the picture. It all comes down to money.

I set about my new job with enthusiasm and vigor, calling record stores across the country and sending them the "new Bill Cosby" record. I spent the next few weeks doing this, mailing the free promo product to the stores and then calling them. Ted rented me a car, and I drove to Newark, New York, Washington, D.C., and Baltimore visiting independent urban record stores. I worked on a few other Nicetown releases, mainly forgettable R&B titles. The Cosby album got some attention but only because Bill Cosby had released a jazz record that was

getting a lot of attention. I definitely took advantage of the retailers' confusion over the two albums that arose to move records. Some retailers thought I was calling about the jazz
release and happily reported Ted's record to the chart editors.

Ted knew how this biz worked, but he just did not get the
part about how you needed records people wanted to hear. I
did not hold that against him, it was just part of who he was.
Truth be told, with the exception of a Bunny Sigler record we
got added to radio, most of the product Ted signed was
forgettable.

My one-room office on the third floor had no heat, which
really sucked in the Philly winter. I had to sit in this freezing
room bundled up in my coat and hat and see my breath as I
spoke with disinterested retailers and program directors about
uninteresting records. One day, as I was on a call, I heard
somebody coming up the stairs, and I assumed it was Ted. Instead, an older gentleman popped in wearing a beautiful cash-
mere coat with an equally nice-looking scarf, hat, and alligator
shoes. He was looking for Ted. Seeing I was on the phone, he
sat down on a stack of boxes and waited while I finished. When
I hung up, he introduced himself: Richard Barrett.

Now at the time, I had no idea who Richard Barrett was. It
was not until later on that I learned Richard had been in the
business a long time and started as an artist in the '50s. He
had a hit song that the Beatles had played as part of their set
in their early days at the Cavern Club in Liverpool. He then
went on to become a producer and discovered Frankie Lymon
and the Teenagers. He had a string of other moderately successful records, but his biggest was a three-girl group called
the Three Degrees. The Three Degrees were a worldwide success, one of the most popular girl groups who came out in the
wake of the Diana Ross & the Supremes phenomenon.

Richard and I talked a while, and I explained what I was doing, showing him my lists of retailers and radio people I was calling and showing him some of my little minor success stories. He was actually impressed—he knew the records were not that great. I told him I knew of artists and groups who, if I had the resources, I could make records with and make it work. Richard stood up and said in his low, raspy voice, "So what's stopping you?"

I explained how Ted did the A&R, and every time I tried to talk to Ted about the records we did, he got incredibly defensive.

Then Richard said something I would carry with me for the rest of my life:

"I would not call anybody about this shit if you paid me a million dollars. There is no amount of money in this world that will buy back your reputation and integrity. When you call these retailers and radio people peddling shit, then you become the shit salesman."

That's when I realized I was earning 120 dollars a week to wreck any type of reputation I was going to build in this business. Richard left, and I sat there, lit a cigarette, and contemplated Richard's advice.

I needed to talk to Ted about a session we had booked for later that day for one of Ted's forgettable artists. While I sat across from Ted, I noticed some twelve-inch records in white sleeves with school bus yellow labels and black magic marker artwork on the labels. I picked one up. It was Schoolly D's "Gangster Boogie" on a label called Place to be Records. I knew who Schoolly was; his track, "Gangster Boogie," was an underground rap sensation in Philly. So, what was Ted doing with it?

Ted noticed me playing with the record.

"Schoolly came to me and wanted me to help him with his career," he said, "but I told him I wasn't interested."

I sat there in disbelief; in this quagmire of shit Ted called a roster, a real artist walked in and Ted told him he wasn't interested?! Whatever transpired between Schoolly and Ted did not surprise me, as Ted probably offered Schoolly some shit deal.

Later that day, while Ted was out, I went into his office and looked through his Rolodex for Schoolly's number. I tucked it away in my pocket for safekeeping.

TED AND I went to the Studio 4 recording studio that day to mix a record. I had been to Studio 4 only once before. The studio was owned and operated by three guys: Joe Nicolo, his twin brother Phil, and Dave Johnson. It was fairly new and located in Old City, an area of mostly vacant old warehouses. In the eighteenth and nineteenth centuries, Philadelphia was a major port on the East Coast. This part of Philadelphia, where Studio 4 was located, was the epicenter of commerce during the Industrial Revolution. The 444 building, in which Studio 4 was housed, was formerly a tanning factory. The business of processing leather in the 1800s was a very nasty undertaking, involving noxious chemicals, urine, and animal excrement to cure hides to create leather goods. Needless to say, the rent was cheap. With money borrowed from family and financing from elsewhere, the partners—Joey, his twin brother Phil, and Dave Johnson—set about building a commercial recording studio. It was the first business in the newly renovated former factory warehouse, which eventually was rented to full capacity by a multitude of different tenants.

Studio 4's success with its recording of the *Nervous Night* album by local rock group the Hooters placed the studio on the map. But Joe and Phil were not just a couple of guys who decided one day to open a studio. Inexperienced people open studios with no real background in an incredibly competitive market with little upside. But the Nicolo brothers were technically gifted from the beginning. As kids in their parents' house, they started learning the art of sound reproduction and constantly endeavored to put their skills to practice. By the time they completed construction of the studio at 444, they were already miles ahead of most studio guys in terms of innovation and technical expertise. They were students of the history of commercial recording, taking cues from Beatles producer George Martin's recording process. Like me, they were Beatles fanatics. I had been a huge Beatles fan all my life, but it was the Nicolo brothers who really gave me an appreciation for George Martin's creative innovations.

The studio was beautiful and designed using interspersed pine over burlap—popular in most professional studios of that period. When Studio 4 opened, Joey was still working a full-time job at Stereo Discounters and was relegated to the night shift, which, at the time, was mainly for hip-hop artists paying smaller recording fees for the off hours. These were considered to be the less desirable projects to work on, as opposed to the rock bands that came in with real recording budgets. Joey, by proxy, became Philadelphia's "go-to guy" for hip-hop production. He recorded and mixed artists like Roxanne Shante for Pop Art Records, Philadelphia's leading hip-hop label, DJ Jazzy Jeff and the Fresh Prince, the Hilltop Hustlers, MC Breeze, and Three Times Dope, as well as numerous other hip-hop artists.

Studio 4 came into prominence as the home of local rock band the Hooters, who recorded their debut album, which went on to sell millions of copies, there. The studio was doing what most studios were doing at the time—local projects, which were their bread and butter.

When Ted and I arrived, it was nighttime. Our engineer, Joe Nicolo, had just got off his day job at Stereo Discounters. We were in the control room. Ted, per usual, hung out for a few minutes to say what he wanted. He boasted about this and that while I sat next to Joe, who I had only met five minutes ago, and rolled my eyes in embarrassment. Ted then left, as he knew I had more studio experience than him, and, frankly, Ted did not have the attention span to focus on a mix for four to five hours. Joey must have seen my expression because the second Ted left Joe turned to me and asked, "How did you end up working for that guy?"

I explained to Joe that Nicetown wasn't my dream job, but I was looking to start my own label.

"So am I," Joe responded. Joe wrote his home phone on the back of a Studio 4 business card, and we agreed to talk. I put the card in my pocket, never imagining the consequences of this chance meeting.

THE NEXT DAY, I called the number for Schoolly that I had pilfered out of Ted's office. After I quickly introduced myself and explained what I did, I offered my help with his career. Schoolly was receptive, and we set up a time for me to come over to his house. I have to admit I was excited, but I was also a little bit apprehensive. Schoolly lived with his mother on Wilton Street, in a row home not unlike the thousands of other single-family dwellings prevalent throughout Philadelphia. I thought I had the ability to help Schoolly take his gig to the next level.

Schoolly's house was about five or six blocks north of the daycare center on a little side street off of Fifty-Second Street. I walked over and knocked on his door. He answered the door with just a towel around his waist. I introduced myself and stuck out my hand. Schoolly looked up and down the street like he was worried about who was watching us and then fixed his eyes.

"I am taking a shower," he said and slammed the door shut.

I stood frozen on Schoolly's porch, stunned by what just occurred. Unsure of what else to do, I walked the five or six blocks back to the daycare center and called Schoolly's number again.

"Call my lawyer, Warren Hamilton," was all Schoolly told me when he answered, but he hung up on me before I could ask for Warren's number. I called directory assistance and asked for Warren Hamilton, Esq. in Philadelphia. Warren and I set up a meeting at his law office in city center. Warren, a criminal defense attorney who had represented Instant Funk, an R&B group, in the seventies but did not have much more experience in the music business beyond that, served many functions for Schoolly—manager, lawyer, etc.

At this point in his career, Schoolly had not done much outside of Philadelphia. I played that angle, thinking I could definitely bring something to the table. I told Warren and Schoolly that we should start a real company set up for the purpose of manufacturing and distributing Schoolly's records. They agreed, and it was with this that I started to disengage from Nicetown and focus on Schoolly full-time.

My meeting with Schoolly could not have happened at a better time; things at Nicetown had been getting worse. Ted had Vince DeRosa's company, Sound Makers, in New Jersey doing his manufacturing. Ted got the idea that if he did a national radio advertising campaign for the Cosby record, it would create enough excitement and groundswell to entice MCA or one of the major labels to pick it up and give Nicetown a distribution deal. This was a lame idea; the record was not that good.

Ted did not have the money to do radio ads. But that did not stop him. Ted set about booking radio advertising for the Cosby record in every major and secondary market, telling the stations to bill Sound Makers for the ad time (Ted had an arrangement with Vince to manufacture and collect from the distributors). Vince knew nothing about this but soon found out. The ads started running. Instead of a groundswell, there were cease and desist letters from Cosby's lawyers and radio stations looking for their money. It got so bad that at one point I just stopped picking up the phone.

I decided at that point that the future of Nicetown Records definitely did not include Nicetown becoming a premier independent R&B label. I grabbed my lists of retailers and radio distributors and walked down the stairs, out the door, and down Fifty-Second Street. Nicetown was now my past; Schoolly was my future.

CHAPTER FOUR

GUCCI TIME

T hings with Schoolly did not get off to a great start. I had started booking him shows in rock clubs because I felt I knew something a lot of people had yet to realize: you could sell hip-hop to white kids.

One of Schoolly's first gigs performing for a predominately white audience was at a club in New Jersey, about two hours away from Philly. It was at this club where I found myself locked in a dressing room backstage while Schoolly and his DJ, Code Money, took refuge in the parking lot, waiting for me. The room was suitably decorated—ripped-up furniture, beer bottles, and cinderblock walls adorned with the magic marker scribbling of a thousand rock bands. The Red Hot Chili Peppers' *Freaky Styley* record thumped through the wall, only slightly muffling the banging on the dressing room door. The banging got louder and more insistent. I was trapped. The club manager and two menacing bouncers stood on the other side of the door. They wanted their money back.

When artists get booked for a gig, they usually take half their money upfront to be held in trust by a booking agent and then collect the other half when they finish their performance. If they are not represented by an agent, they get paid after the performance. But, at Schoolly's insistence, I demanded the other half of Schoolly's fee before he even took the stage. This was unheard of and unwelcome news for the club manager, who had to count out the cash from the door receipts, which were considerable and took time away from the performance. The crowd grew restless, as some had traveled long distances to see Schoolly perform and didn't appreciate having to wait even longer.

After Schoolly performed five songs, which is a typical early eighties hip-hop set, the audience, being used to the hour-plus set rock bands performed, became outraged. Code started tearing down his turntables. The club manager yelled at me, demanding Schoolly get back on stage. I rushed to the dressing room to talk to Schoolly, the club manager and bouncers right behind me. I asked them to wait outside. I walked in, locked the door, and turned around to find out the room was empty.

Schoolly had already left the venue.

I was trapped in that room with no way out. What if the manager and the bouncers walked in and discovered that Schoolly and Code had already left? Things would get unpleasant. I looked around the windowless dressing room, and my eyes fell on an air conditioner positioned at the top of the wall, just inches below the ceiling. I dragged a coffee table over and stood on top of it. The air conditioner was wedged in pretty solid but had some play. I pulled it toward me and got a face full of disgusting brown stagnant water that had gathered inside it. I lifted out the unit and placed it on the coffee table. With one foot on the table, I placed the other on the unit and pushed myself up to the now-gaping hole in the wall. I crawled head first through the opening and fell on top of a dumpster, startling a group of club patrons smoking weed behind the club.

Schoolly's Lincoln was gone. Fuck! Please tell me he did not leave me here in Passaic, New Jersey, to get the shit knocked out of me by the club employees who thought he just fucked them. Perhaps they parked up front? I ran up the side of the building to the front and looked around the corner to see a huge crowd complaining and yelling about getting their money back. Just then, the manager, bouncers, and bar-backs came crashing through the front entrance, running in the opposite direction of where I stood, running toward the parking lot on the other side of the building. I walked past the crowd.

"You're bleeding!" a girl said to me, pointing at a big red splotch on my shirt. I had cut myself while climbing out of the hole.

I ignored her, closed my jean jacket, and walked out into the street, dodging traffic. I walked about three blocks thinking about how I was going to get home. Where the fuck did Schoolly go? This was before the dawn of cellular phones. I had no way to contact him. Did he really leave me?

Just as I began to curse his very existence and curse myself for creating this predicament, a white Lincoln Continental pulled up. The driver, Big Al, hopped into the passenger side, and I got into the driver's side. Schoolly and Code were already asleep in the back seat. Big Al handed me a bag with burgers and fries. I put the car in drive and made a U-turn, driving away from the club. In the rearview mirror, I saw a police car pulling into the club parking lot.

I had some time to think on this ride home. After about twenty minutes I calmed down. Schoolly, Code, and Big Al were crashed. This gig was a disaster. The club was too small, and Schoolly's set wasn't long enough. Rock fans wanted the performance to be an hour long, but in hip-hop in the early eighties, the artist did an average of three to five songs. Hip-hop was permeated by independent promoters who often stiffed artists, which was why Schoolly would not take the stage unless he was paid in full up front.

Rock promoters do not operate like that. They have reputations to protect, and stiffing bands would make them *persona non grata* to the booking agents. Indie hip-hop promoters, however, for the most part did not bother about such things. They were more interested in quick one-off scores and did not see promoting hip-hop shows as career building blocks. How could I reconcile these two worlds to create something legitimate? I needed to get a real booking agent for Schoolly and start him on a conventional tour.

By the spring of 1985, things were put into motion for Schoolly. We pressed up the first singles under the Schoolly D Records label, of which I was getting four hundred dollars a week to manage. We had just released the singles "PSK" and "Gucci Time." I set up manufacturing with Sound Makers and made arrangements with independent distributors to pay half of the costs of C.O.D. when they receive shipments. At one point, I drove to Encore Distributors in Queens with a car full of records and slept in the car overnight in the parking lot to deliver the records and collect a check. This was the only way to get records made. In the years to come, Schoolly D would be heralded as the pioneer of what was to become known as

"Gangster Rap," but right now, he trusted nobody when it came to money. Schoolly had a tough time investing in his own business. When we needed records pressed, I could barely get him to write a check for the amount needed.

One day, I went into Downtown Records, a store in Manhattan, to see if they were carrying the "PSK" and "Gucci Time" singles. As expected, they were. Except there was an issue.

The labels on the singles were exactly like ours at Schoolly D Records, except they said, "Distributed by Warlock Records." I brought one to the counter to complain about the bootleg copy to the cashier. The guy sitting behind the counter appeared to be in his sixties, was smoking a cigar, and seemed totally disinterested. As I left the store, the guy at the counter said, "Warlock can at least get the records pressed and delivered." I fumed.

Once I got back to Philly, Schoolly and I drove to Sound Makers. We pulled in and, as we parked, Schoolly revealed a gun under his jacket. I panicked.

"This is not how we want to play this."

"This is how I'm playing it!" Schoolly responded.

I asked him to just chill until we knew the facts. We went in and asked for Vince. Vince came out, looked at us quizzically, and asked to talk to Schoolly alone. They disappeared for a bit, and then Schoolly came back carrying his tape masters. We got in the car, and I peppered him with questions about what happened. Vince said he had to get Warlock Records to "help him collect" from some distributors. I was not sure about that as I could not imagine any distributor not paying Vince. Schoolly also said that Vince had told him to get rid of me. Gee, I wonder why? We were done with Sound Makers. We needed a different way to get records out.

The "Gucci Time" and "PSK" singles became underground

hip-hop anthems and went on to inspire West Coast artists Ice-T and Eazy-E. They had a sound unlike any other. These tracks were done in a little eight-track studio that recorded the Philadelphia Orchestra, and the bass drum, snare, and high-hat were put through a plate reverb, giving it a cavernous booming sound. These recordings brought Schoolly worldwide acclaim.

But I was having trouble getting these singles pressed due to lack of funds. A company in Newark, New Jersey, called Peter Pan Records, manufactured and distributed children's records. Now, Schoolly D's records were about as far from a children's record as possible, but I called them up nonetheless and made an appointment to meet with them. In November of 1985, I drove out to their facility and showed them everything they needed to know about Schoolly, including open orders from distributors all over the country. I sat with them and, over Chinese food, we made a deal. They would manufacture and distribute our records.

Things were coming along quite nicely at this point. We had all moved out of the house in West Philly. Rich Murray had moved to NYC to work in film. Jeff Coulter got a place with his girlfriend, Amy, and I crashed at my father's apartment in Strafford, Pennsylvania, after my parents separated. At this point I occasionally drank beer, but beyond that I had pretty much not partaken in drug use since using amphetamines in the service. But now I was introduced to a new drug which gave me incredible energy, especially since Black Beauties weren't available. I had started using methamphetamine, or simply "meth." I had dated some go-go dancers who used it, and I found it readily available and cheap. This gig took a lot of energy. Things were not always easy. Working as Schoolly D's manager and label was like following an elephant with a broom. He had a real knack for pissing people off, and I was the designated shit catcher. I did it with great enthusiasm because, to me, the music was beyond anything that was on the radio. It was truly cutting edge and authentic. There was nothing else like it.

Earlier, before I was involved, Schoolly's lawyer, Warren Hamilton, signed Schoolly to a booking agent in New York. I was not satisfied with the meager amount of shows Schoolly was getting and called the agent, Ritchie Walters, to express my misgiving about Schoolly's future with his agency. Ritchie asked me to come to New York and have lunch. When I arrived at the offices, he was warm and cordial. Ritchie basically broke it down for me. An agent can book shows but cannot single-handedly create demand for the artist. This is incumbent upon the label as well. He could book tours, but who would pay the tour support to help Schoolly D get out there? After spending time with Ritchie, I came to some conclusions.

First, I realized that Schoolly wasn't a big enough artist for me to threaten pulling him from the agency. I need to create the demand for him, and simply having a booking agent would not make promoters want to book Schoolly. You can have every part of the puzzle but there still needs to be a defining event, something that might look insignificant at the time but would have immense ramifications. For me, and for Schoolly, that event happened almost a year later in October of 1986.

SPIN **MAGAZINE WAS** started by Bob Guccione Jr., son of *Penthouse* magazine founder Bob Guccione. *Spin* magazine was the Gen X alternative to *Rolling Stone*. Inside the glossy pages of its October issue was a half-page article about Schoolly with a photo of Schoolly and Code Money standing amongst residents of his Parkside neighborhood. The *Spin* article created a wave of interest in Schoolly, which I was all too happy to capitalize on. The article was written by John Leland, a music journalist who had called the phone number on the single and asked if he could come to Philly with a photographer.

After the *Spin* article, I successfully took Schoolly from a regional artist to a national one, getting his records to distributors, retailers, and DJs in every market. This was a lot easier said than done. While we had zero commercial radio play, there was one crucial thing I learned early on: White kids love hip-hop. Or at least, they love Schoolly D.

When white club DJs in the States played "PSK" and "Gucci Time," the dance floor was packed. This soon caught the attention of DJs in London. Soon enough, we were approached by an independent label in London, Rhythm King, which was distributed through Daniel Miller's Mute Records, home of artists Depeche Mode, Erasure, and the Silicone Teens. We used the advance from Rhythm King to put together Schoolly's first album, known thereafter as the Yellow album or the "PSK" album.

Then things really started to heat up. We were selling records. We performed to bigger audiences, with artists like the Beastie Boys opening up for Schoolly. We did a tour in Europe opening up for Big Audio Dynamite, the band formed by former Clash guitarist Mick Jones.

I learned a lot about the record business in those years—reading business trade publications, picking up information from everyone I came across. But, more than ever before, I wanted to start my own label. I had held on to the Studio 4 business card that Joe Nicolo had given me a few years back. It was time to put my dream into motion; I called him up one afternoon, and we set up a time to meet at Studio 4.

In December of 1986, I met Joey Nicolo in Studio 4's parking lot at 444 North Third Street on a Sunday afternoon. Our game plan was simple. We talked about creating a "full service" label. He would oversee the production of product, and I would be responsible for the manufacturing, distribution, marketing, and promotion. At this point I did not have any inclinations to be a producer, unlike when I was hanging out with Frank Virtue. Frank's studio was a professional 24-track commercial facility, but it was old. With computers starting to become part of the studio process and giving traditional 24-track studios infinite tracking capabilities, modern production was now on a whole new level. This technology was daunting for the technically challenged, like me. Besides that, I did not have the patience to spend countless hours in one place listening to the same track hundreds of times in a row.

Now, there are some partnerships and companies that called themselves a record label by virtue of the fact that the end product had their logo on it. In actuality, these companies were really just production entities. For the most part, they sign artists and record them, but the bulk of the process of setting up a record for manufacturing, distribution, marketing, and promotion is handled by either a larger third-party label or distributor. An example here is a prospective producer who signs an artist and records his record and then does a production deal with a bigger independent label, who, in turn, has a deal with an independent distributor or major label entity. If the record becomes a hit, then many entities step on the money as it slowly trickles to the originating production company, and very little ends up with the artist. We did not want this. We wanted to do everything, soup to nuts. At first, we called our new entity Pyramid Productions. I had no idea how we could have ever come up with such an ambiguous name. I was still very much committed to Schoolly.

In June of 1987, Schoolly opened for the Red Hot Chili Peppers in L.A. During this time, while on a break at the Tropicana hotel, I received a phone call poolside from movie producer Jon Avnet. He wanted Schoolly to be in a film he was producing called Less Than Zero. The next day, we went to the film location and Schoolly and Code filmed a performance scene in a club during which Andrew McCarthy's character looks for Robert Downey Jr.'s character. The footage of Schoolly was later cut from the film during editing. It was not until years later that I would eventually see this film—about a guy who starts a record label and becomes a drug addict—and chuckle at the irony of the whole thing.

One day, Joey and I were sitting in the office of our attorney, Arthur Mann. While Arthur was on a phone call, Joey picked up a cassette by some unknown rock group called Roughhouse. Joey said Roughhouse would be a cool name for a label. I agreed, especially since the irony was I actually grew up in a rough house. But I suggested we change the spelling of rough to "ruff" to make it more in keeping with the street vernacular. And, so, in July of 1987, Ruffhouse was born.

My first office was actually a vestibule, or a triangle-shaped room separating the newly built Studio 4 B-room from the hallway. It had enough room for a desk (made up of a few pieces of plywood covered in black-and-red vinyl), a lamp, and an old princess phone Joe brought in from home. It did not take long for the word to get out in Philly that Schoolly D's manager started a new record label with Joe "The Butcher" Nicolo at Studio 4. Soon, every aspiring rap artist from Philadelphia, New Jersey, and Delaware made his way to Studio 4 to get a record deal. As the throngs of kids who showed up unannounced became a logistical nightmare, we realized we were definitely not set up for this. To get to my office, I had to push my way past kids lined up in the stairwell, with the line overflowing out into the hallway. It was not a very good way to start the day. It became disruptive and distracting. We also learned it could be dangerous.

In New York City, a multitude of labels were available for artists. In Philadelphia at the time, however, besides Pop Art Records, we were the only game in town. An aspiring hip-hop artist would get out of bed in the morning and think to themselves, "I am going to Ruffhouse today to get a record deal." When it does not come to fruition, often there is anger, accusations of racism, and violence. I have been threatened on many occasions and told that, because I am white, I don't know what I am talking about.

We quickly established certain days of the week for us to listen to the more promising artists perform live in the studio. During this audition, they sang or rapped through the microphones, and we listened to them in the control room. But the tides of artists with their demos kept showing up unannounced, regardless of the designated days, which finally led us to setting up a real office.

Our first official Ruffhouse office was a large, cinderblock room with a double sliding glass door next to Studio 4. It was formerly a video production company run by a guy named Chris Yeworth. Chris's father was a B movie director who directed *The Blob*, starring a young Steve McQueen in the '50s. What I liked about the space was that it had a partition at the door so visitors had to stop at a desk before they could just walk in.

I spent one Sunday cleaning it out and painting the walls white and painting black-and-red trim to match the new Ruffhouse logo. A young street artist designed our new logo and painted it on the wall. It was a funky logo done in cartoonish graffiti-style lettering—popular at the time. All in all, it was a very cool office.

I brought Jeff Coulter on to help me set up the label infrastructure. He was very computer savvy and helped me organize my mailing lists of radio mix show DJs, club DJs, record pools, and retailers.

We could not afford a phone system, so the guy from the phone company hooked us up with what was called a "hunt system." We had multiple phones with one number. If a call came in, one phone would ring. If somebody was on that phone, then the call would go to the next phone, and so forth. Each phone's cord went to a jack that was attached to a piece of plywood that was duct-taped to one of the legs of my desk. Not very attractive, but it worked. At one point we had about eight phones with phone lines running every which way throughout the office. Sometimes, when the phone rang while there were multiple people on different phones, whoever was answering would frantically go from phone to phone to see which one was ringing. One minor miscalculation was putting that number on the Schoolly D records and some of our earlier releases. The phone rang nonstop, mainly from aspiring artists looking to get signed. As we grew, the phone system became absurd. However, there were a lot of calls that were great opportunities. Major label heads, A&R guys, movie producers, distributors, promoters, radio programmers, DJs, and journalists were blowing that number up.

Despite the mismatched furniture and crazy phone system, this office was the closest thing I had to a home. I was living like a vagabond, staying at different places all over the city. My clothes were at apartments of different girls or the apartments of my various buddies. I ended up sleeping at Ruffhouse many a night after being out. For me, Ruffhouse was purpose, chaos, and adventure.

It was an interesting time in the music business. Not since the fifties had it been viable for an independent label to have a hit record without the machinations of major label distribution. In the eighties, there were five major distribution entities: WEA (Warner-Atlantic-Electra), CBS (Columbia and Epic), CEMA (Capitol-EMI-Angel-Verve-Chrysalis), MCA (MCA, PolyGram, Mercury, Motown, Island), and RCA (RCA, Arista, Jive). These five companies had their own manufacturing and distribution and were situated worldwide. But there was a slew of independents: Tommy Boy, Sleeping Bag, Emergency Records, Next Plateau, 4th & Broadway, Priority Records, as well as countless others.

Hip-hop music became a growing juggernaut, with independent labels selling hundreds of thousands of records. Most of these labels were fiercely independent, and for good reason. The manufacturing and distribution costs were small, and that combined with the low-cost, high-impact of cultural lifestyle marketing made being an independent label very lucrative. An indie label did not have the overhead of a major, so the profit margins were notable; but at the same time, an indie had to be much more careful because it could not afford to take the risks of a major. A lot of indie labels were one record away from getting shut down or absorbed by a bigger label. One of the key problems for independent start-ups was getting paid by the distributor. By the eighties, there were roughly fifteen independent distributors of note. Most of these companies had been around since the heyday of the independent record business. They made the least amount of money in the whole process among everybody concerned, including the record company, manufacturer, and retailer.

A newly established label needed to have multiple releases over a period of time in order to get paid consistently. For example, a new label shipping out a record that becomes a hit would obviously want to get paid, but when the distributor pays the label and then later gets hit with "returns" (records that do not sell), then the distributor gets stuck holding the bag if there are no additional releases from the label for the distributor to charge against the returns of the first release. Often, the distributor calls the label only to find out the number is disconnected. This scenario has caused most independent distributors to take a very cynical view of newly minted independent labels. Distributors will usually not start paying regularly until there is a pipeline of records coming from the label.

Hip-hop was an exciting new revenue source with very low production costs. The major labels were drawn to these easy profits. The younger major label A&R (Artists & Repertoire) representatives were soon looking for hip-hop artists, and Schoolly D was a prime catch. As his representative, I was courted by every major label and had meetings in New York and L.A.

The stumbling block was we were not shopping Schoolly as an artist but rather as a label. I had a meeting at Capitol Records with A&R executives Tom Whalley and Tim Devine, who told me their reluctance to enter into an arrangement like this was due to Schoolly virtually being the only artist on the label, although we had done some other releases under the Schoolly D label moniker with artists like Robbie B and DJ Jazz, Royal Ron, and Pimp Pretty. Schoolly D was the only artist of note, and the label did not have the track record to justify a co-venture multi-artist distribution deal. But that did not stop me from trying.

We had just completed the *Saturday Night* record with Joey

engineering and mixing. It was a hip-hop masterpiece and sold in droves. As usual, the distribution became troublesome due to a lack of manufacturing funds. I wanted Schoolly D to remain an independent artist with his own label, but truth be told, he did not have the discipline for it. He was young and could not envision investing in the future. The offers from the majors were significant. I was making four hundred dollars a week working for Schoolly, which, in fact, was a pittance given the scope of my responsibilities. I was tired of swimming against the tide, and I thought, at that point, Schoolly was looking for that big check that only a major label could write. So, in the end, in September of 1987, we went with Jive Records.

The founders of the company, Clive Calder and Ralph Simon, were from South Africa. They came to London and formed a company called Zomba Group, which was the umbrella company for their different endeavors. Under Zomba Group, there was Jive Records (the label), Zomba Music (the publishing company), Battery Sound (their recording studios), and Dream Hire (their outboard gear rental company). They made an immediate impact in the hip-hop market, signing groups like Boogie Down Productions, Whodini, A Tribe Called Quest, Kool Moe Dee, and DJ Jazzy Jeff and the Fresh Prince. These signings were mostly due to Barry Weiss, the U.S. president of Jive Records. Barry grew up in the record business and was exceptionally talented. His father, Hy Weiss, was an industry legend. At the time, the New York Jive offices were located in a townhouse on the Upper East Side. Although the offices were small and crowded, the label packed a lethal punch. They were distributed by RCA, one of the major distribution powers, and the company was enjoying major success in hip-hop.

Within just days of signing the agreement with Jive, I got off a Virgin Air flight from London at Newark airport and went right to the clubs in Philly. I had just returned from Europe where Schoolly had done a headline tour. He was on the cover of every music magazine in the United Kingdom and Europe, including *NME* (*New Music Express*) and *Melody Maker*. I was out for most of the night and into the early morning hours. When I entered the studio's control room to greet Joe the next morning, I had not slept at all.

A studio intern came in and said I had a phone call. I picked up the phone and a girl with an English accent confirmed I was on the line. She put me on hold, and I was transferred to a speakerphone. On the other end of the line, a group of angry English executives from Rhythm King (the English record company distributing the Schoolly records in Europe) were yelling—at me. They had just learned of Schoolly's defection to Jive Records.

Jive Records had wasted no time in getting out a press release announcing their signing of Schoolly D to a worldwide deal. I was going to call Rhythm King later that day as I did not think they would know about it yet. I knew they were going to be pissed, but I was not prepared for this avalanche of piss-tivity. But then, after I had thought about it, I didn't blame them. But at the same time I also thought since the deal with Rhythm King was only for two records outside of North America, it was obvious that Schoolly was going to sign with a major at some point. It was inevitable, and I was sure Rhythm King knew this.

In November of 1987, a local rock group called the Dead Milkmen had a modern rock radio hit called "Punk Rock Girl." The group was signed to a company in L.A. called Enigma Entertainment Group. Enigma was a label and distribution company for alternative and obscure indie labels and bands. They got their start with metal bands, such as Stryper and Poison. Enigma was distributed by Capitol-EMI.

The owners of Enigma reached out to me via the managers for the Dead Milkmen to offer Ruffhouse a distribution deal. Although the partners who owned Enigma had no particular affinity for hip-hop, they, like a lot of companies, saw the burgeoning market and wanted a taste. We were very excited. Enigma flew Joe and me out to L.A. The deal called for them to give us fifty thousand dollars a year for overhead and a commitment to release three artists a year.

Our first signing was a female rapper named Mac-Money. She was a Philly battle rapper who had previously done an answer record to Schoolly's "PSK." The record we did with her was probably the most credible record we did under the deal with Enigma. Mac-Money, by local hip-hop standards, was exceptional and could have probably done well beyond the region although the writing was not there. We did some other records through Enigma, but none of them came to much consequence, and our time with Enigma quickly came to a close. There was too much of a cultural clash. Enigma was a label whose repertoire was alternative rock, much of it promoted via the college radio microcosm. Hip-hop was too alien for their marketing and sales staff. At this time, Pop Art had done a deal with Jive, giving them major label distribution. Joe and I realized we needed that same muscle. Little did we know that opportunity was on the front porch about to knock.

CHAPTER FIVE

THE BIG RED MACHINE

B y March of 1988, I found myself with my hands full. Apart from managing Schoolly, I also took on a Philadelphia techno-rock band called the Executive Slacks, who did a remake of Gary Glitter's "Rock and Roll" on their *Fire & Ice* album. I did a twelve-inch remix of this track and released it to notable acclaim from DJs and licensed it overseas. But the band had problems. The original lead singer, Matt Marello, left the band to move to New York to be a painter, leaving a creative deficit in the group. The new singer was good, but the group's core audience did not embrace him. But, for me, I found the drummer's personality to be very disagreeable. When the Executive Slacks decided they wanted to fire me as their manager, they saved me the awkward scenario of quitting.

I had my hands full, sure, but I was not really making any money. But soon this was about to change. It was about this time that I had what was probably my first real relationship since Robin. Her name was Rose Mann (no relation to Arthur Mann, our attorney). I had met her one night at a club, and we hit it off. She was from New Jersey and had just broken up with her boyfriend. We started hanging out, going to the movies, and visiting her family in New Jersey on the weekends. I really liked her family—she had an older brother and sister who married spouses who were also brother and sister. They were born-again Christians, and the two brothers-in-law were both ministers at their respective churches. One of them lived on a farm in Jersey with their children, and when we visited, I really enjoyed hanging out with them. Although I was in the business of selling hip-hop and they were devout in their beliefs, they never once disparaged my chosen profession and were extremely cool to hang out with. Rose and I got an apartment together at Second and Brown Street, about five blocks from the studio. Rose helped out in the office making calls to retail stores. She had quite a talent for it and would eventually become a key part of Ruffhouse's marketing and promotion team in the years to come. I was told by one retailer that Rose was a breath of fresh air because she was not jaded like most retail marketing reps were.

Apart from the Enigma deal and the artist management, I was doing marketing and promotion for other labels. I would enlist Rose and a woman named Jackie Paul to help me. Jackie was the Rap chart editor for *Impact* magazine, a trade magazine for black radio. Jackie talked to all of the mix show DJs and radio programmers across the country to compile the list for the top performing hip-hop albums and songs. *Impact* came out biweekly with a yearly convention, which Rose and I attended a few times.

We worked a score of records, including Eazy-E and NWA for Priority, Tone Lōc and Young MC for Island Records, and many others. Soon, I started amassing gold and platinum records hanging on the wall. Major label reps who wanted to sign Schoolly were then approaching me about their new hip-hop signings and seeking my help in promoting them. The success of Schoolly D and Jazzy Jeff and the Fresh Prince made Joe one of the most sought-after mix engineers in hip-hop. At one point, ten of the top fifty hip-hop songs on the charts were mixed by Joe or promoted by me. Between A&R, production, marketing, and promotion, we were at the top of the game.

At this point in time, I was using meth as a coping tool to get through having what I felt were multiple jobs: managing Schoolly D and all that entailed, building Ruffhouse, and running an independent marketing-promotion company. I was also promoting live shows at the TLA and the Chestnut Cabaret. Very rarely would I do cocaine, and that was only when I went out with friends. I really could not afford coke. But meth was cheap; I knew a few strip clubs where it was always available. A lot of the go-go dancers used it to keep them going through their shifts. It could keep you up for days, which for me at the time was good because I never slowed down, and I did not sleep a lot. My childhood internal clock set to always be up before sunrise to avoid certain members of my family followed me until I had joined the Navy, but even then, I only had an average of about five hours of broken sleep. Some nights I just stayed up through sunrise.

One day that winter, I had a call from Rick Chertoff, a staff producer at Columbia who had been working at Studio 4 on the Tommy Conwell record. Rick had produced the Hooters albums and had signed and produced Cyndi Lauper. The hallways of the 444 Building concourse on any given day were filled with boxes of records being sent via UPS to radio, clubs, and retail. Rick would see all this activity and occasionally pop into the Ruffhouse office and talk about the label.

Rick asked if Joe and I could come up to Columbia Records for a meeting. CBS was arguably the largest record company in the world with its Columbia Records label originating in the 1800s. It was frequently referred to within the industry as "The Big Red Machine," due to its "iconic" red album labels and its ability to move "tonnage" when it came to selling records. CBS had created the concept of building their own manufacturing and distribution system, a template that was followed by Warner Brothers, EMI, MCA, and RCA.

Having a wholly owned manufacturing and distribution mechanism is what defined these companies as "majors." CBS's Columbia label was the home to some of the greatest artists in recorded music history: Bob Dylan, Bruce Springsteen, Barbra Streisand, Miles Davis, and Frank Sinatra. CBS also created the "LP"—long-playing 33 and 1/3 vinyl formats. They had offered it to RCA as a joint venture project, but RCA's legendary founder, Robert Sarnoff, turned them down, believing the format would never catch on.

On the day of the meeting, I drove to Newark where I could park for free and take the path train into the city, which was then 95 cents. I transferred to a subway to go to Midtown. Getting off on Fifth Avenue, I walked to the 51 West Fifty-Second Street address of the storied "Black Rock" building, home of CBS. The Columbia Broadcast System group of companies included CBS Records, the umbrella organization of both the Columbia and Epic record labels.

Joe did not accompany me for this meeting. I approached this building with excitement and trepidation. This was it. The large monolithic black glass and steel structure with the gold letters CBS above the revolving door was the culmination of everything I'd worked toward since I walked out of the gates of the Naval Air Station in California. Ruffhouse could finally have the backing of a major, much like what Jive had with RCA. I walked to the reception and told security I had an appointment with Rick Chertoff. They gave me a stick-on pass, and I was directed to an elevator that looked like a gold-plated bank vault. At the eleventh floor, a woman took me to Rick's office. I had been to the offices of major labels before, but CBS was different; it had the atmosphere of power.

Rick greeted me, and we took a stairwell up one floor to the twelfth floor. In the executive office area, we entered into the office of Don Ienner, the newly appointed president of Columbia Records. "Donnie," as his friends called him, was not what I had expected. I anticipated a group of older guys wearing three-piece suits in a wood paneled corporate office, but Donnie was in his thirties. He was gregarious and confident—a real record guy. I was wearing a suit for this meeting, and Donnie was wearing jeans and a white button-down polo shirt. Donnie was not alone in his office. He was sitting on his desk talking with CBS Records president Tommy Mottola, who wore a blue polo, sport coat, and tie. I was also introduced to six or seven other executives, a mix of other Columbia Records department heads and CBS business affairs people.

The room was spacious with a sectional couch that went around two walls occupied by the other executives. Rick sat on the couch, and I went to sit next to him, but Tommy held me back and directed me to a chair in front of Donnie's desk. The chair faced everybody. I was not prepared for this scenario where I was addressing eight or nine people.

Tommy took a seat. "Chris," he said, "tell us what you have been up to."

I realized then I was mistaken in my original perception of this meeting. I thought it was a meeting with Rick and Donnie when, in fact, it turned out to be me addressing a group of traditional industry guys on the development of hip-hop music and street culture marketing. In this moment, everything I'd been doing in my life up until that point felt like an unanswered question and now was my opportunity to finally answer it.

I talked for a good thirty minutes on how I set up regional street teams for promoting hip-hop records and all of my nontraditional marketing methodologies, working independent retail, mix shows, clubs, and lifestyle marketing in general. I said if I told a retailer or DJ I was sending him a record, I did not wait until I did a mass mailing as most people do. I sent it out right then and there. I said I treated these retailers and DJs like gold. I finished talking and sort of sat there for a minute and Donnie asked me who my lawyer was.

Before I could verbalize a response, Donnie and Tommy stood up to shake my hand and said, "Welcome to Columbia Records."

Someone could have ten lifetimes in the music business and still not have a moment like this. It was beyond description. I was still processing what happened when Rick walked me to the elevator. Although I was already in the record business, having a distribution with Columbia Records legitimized me, especially in the eyes of my father. It wasn't that I was looking for my father's approval; he always seemed supportive and had actually recommended early on that I should move to L.A. to be in the hub of the entertainment business. While my father was proud of me, even after I had hit records, certain family members talked shit about me every chance they could get. A few months before, at my brother Robert's wedding, my brother, John, gleefully told me the family members on the West Coast had come to the conclusion I was a flake, and the consensus was my music business pursuits were a pipe dream. He was especially happy to tell me my father was in agreement. But having a contract from Columbia/CBS dispelled all of that.

The initial agreement called for CBS to give us one hundred twenty-five thousand dollars overhead for the first year with yearly increments to follow. That was the largest sum of money either Joe or I had ever seen. On top of that, we received budgets to sign artists and make records. But once the euphoria subsided, a sobering reality set in. We needed to make records.

We had a deal with CBS, but I had nowhere to live. My relationship with Rose had been deteriorating over time. She was one of the most loving human beings on earth, but she had a very low tolerance for my drinking, combined with a suspicious nature when it came to other women. Whenever we went out socializing, Rose convinced herself I was somehow romantically involved with any woman we met, be it somebody's girlfriend or a coat-check girl at a nightclub. My relationship with Rose became untenable, especially when she started to accuse me of having affairs with female colleagues in the record business who I had never even met in person but talked to on the phone for work. After a while, Rose and I called it quits, but she remained a valuable part of the Ruffhouse machine. She had across-the-board relationships with retailers in every market, and she could get a record onto the retail charts. We ended up becoming closer as friends rather than lovers. When I moved out of the apartment, I did not have a place to live; I was a vagabond, crashing at different people's apartments and houses in the city.

But I did own something. In spring of 1988 I bought my first car, a 1986 Jaguar XJ6, cobalt blue with a doe-skin interior. That was the start of my never-ending love affair with English luxury cars. Joe and the other guys at Studio 4 saw me as a bit of a spendthrift who went out and bought a luxury car but did not have a place to live. But I was not thinking about my domestic situation; Ruffhouse was my home, and the label was my family. Joe was my best friend; I did not need domesticity. The concept of having the home with a wife and kids, like my colleagues had, seemed alien to me. Just about every night I hung out at nightclubs and the barely legal after-hours social clubs. I was going to stay single, or at least I thought I was.

From the start, Studio 4 had an intern program in conjunction with Temple University. Joe and his twin, Phil, were both alumni of Temple University's famed Radio, Television, and Film program. Students in this program worked at Studio 4 getting practical experience in a commercial recording studio while earning college credit toward their degree. One day, a woman showed up at the studio for the intern program from Temple. She was tall and thin with jet-black hair with bangs. She looked like a European model, and I was immediately drawn to her. Her name was Myrna Jordan. Myrna came into the Ruffhouse office to ask for something from one of the staff. I introduced myself and asked if she wanted to walk to the bank with me. I could not have been more obvious, but I couldn't help myself. She agreed.

Myrna was from Kentucky. She left in her last year of school at the University of Kentucky to move up to Philadelphia with her band, Zuzu's Petals, to give it a go at success. The band consisted of her brother, Bob, her then-boyfriend, Robbie Rizzo, and childhood friend Tim Reeder. They originally talked about moving to New York but decided Philadelphia's lower cost of living and its close proximity to New York made it a more practical base of operations for the band. They did some shows around Philadelphia, but eventually Myrna quit the group to focus on the film business. She decided to finish getting her degree in film and television from Temple University. I asked her out, and she said she had a boyfriend. I somehow had a feeling this wasn't entirely true and that she was trying to let me off easily. Myrna spent a few weeks at Studio 4 and left.

Six months later, Myrna's name came up in a conversation with a mutual friend who gave me her phone number. I called her, and we went on a date to an Italian restaurant in Narberth. When I dropped her off, I did not even get a goodnight kiss. This was going to be work. But after months of courting, we ended up getting an apartment together on the penthouse floor of a building on City Line Avenue overlooking the city.

Not long into our new relationship with Columbia, I received a phone call from a guy in L.A. named Len Fico. Len was an all-purpose music guy; he did some management and set up deals. He told me about an artist named Cheba who had a track called "The Piper." It was a hip-hop rendition of the Pied Piper children's story. It was clever, with Cheba doing different voices of characters in the story. This was going to be our first single on Ruffhouse through our deal with Columbia. We did a "singles deal," meaning we agreed to do one song while retaining the option to do either additional singles or an album should the first single make enough noise in the market. The song was on a cassette, and we were told the location of the actual studio multi-tracks was being located.

After we did the contract, it became apparent the multi-track tapes were either lost or stolen. No problem, we could replicate the song and just have Cheba come to our studio and redo the track. Joe set about redoing the track, which was not much of a challenge as it was a very simple production. He replicated it to a tee. We flew Cheba in from L.A. He was a really nice guy who told me about all of the artists he hung out with, like Whodini and Digital Underground. At the time, Digital Underground had a huge song called "The Humpty Dance." Shock G was the creative force behind Digital Underground, whose members included a young Tupac Shakur. "The Humpty Dance" featured Shock G performing as his alter ego persona Humpty dressing up in outlandish pimp attire with a false groucho nose.

When we went into the studio with Cheba to cut his vocal performance for "The Piper" track, we got a big surprise. For reasons unknown to us at that time, Cheba's performance on "The Piper" did not sound anything like the demo we'd heard. He could rap, but his performance lacked the timbre, color, and animation of the vocal featured on the original tape.

After some investigation, Cheba finally admitted he did not perform the original vocal nor did he write it. Instead, it was written and performed by Shock G from Digital Underground. According to Cheba, Shock G "gave him" the demo to go out and shop it for himself as an artist.

This was bad news.

We signed an artist through our first deal with Columbia on a song that he did not write or perform based on a demo everybody loved. Joe and I made the decision that we would not let this crash the ship. To recover, we had Cheba do the song painstakingly word-by-word until Joe—with editing and determination—got it to sound exactly like the demo. It was not easy, and it took a great deal of time, but Joe persevered, and the song was finished. No one outside of our small circle knew the backstory.

Next, we had to get a mechanical license from Shock G. This proved to be quite the task. Although we had repeated assurances from Cheba that there would be no issues with Shock G, we would not move forward until we had this piece of paper in our hands. I called Digital Underground's manager, Atron Gregory.

"No problem," he said. "Just fax it, and I'll get Shock G to sign it."

It was not like Joe and I committed fraud. Artists had been doing records written by other people since the dawn of the business. We scheduled the single and moved ahead. I got Rich Murray to come down from New York to do the video on a very small budget. Everyone loved the video and the song.

But we had a small problem. Weeks had gone by, and we had yet to receive the license back from Atron. But, based on his word, not Cheba's, we moved ahead with the single release. The video was scheduled for release along with the twelve-inch record. We delivered the master elements to CBS with the video. Desperate to button up the issue, I talked to Atron and explained the situation. He seemed to understand and asked me to refax him the document. He sounded as though it was just a matter of getting a minute to sit down with Shock G and having him sign it. Understandable, as they had a hit record and were on tour with a hectic schedule. He did acknowledge that Shock G gave Cheba the demo to shop and there would not be a problem. However, with Shock G being the writer, CBS needed a copy of the mechanical license as part of delivery requirements.

Finally, with no time to spare, I jumped on a plane to where Digital Underground was performing in Chicago. I went to their hotel, called Atron, and waited in the lobby. After about two hours, Atron got off the elevator with the document in hand, signed.

This single was quite a journey overall, but Joe and I learned a valuable lesson from this: Never again would we sign an artist unseen.

Cheba's single came out and sold over twenty-five thousand copies—nothing to really celebrate but not a total failure. We did not move on to an album, but we had just enough encouragement based on retail and video play to do another single.

Cheba talked often about Teena Marie and how they were good friends. He said that Teena would do a feature vocal for him. Down the hall from us was a studio owned by musician/producer Jim Salamone. Jim worked with a lot of Philly artists, like LeVert and Grover Washington Jr., the celebrated jazz saxophonist. Grover was a mainstay at R&B radio, and we thought it would be cool to do a Cheba record featuring Grover Washington Jr. and Teena Marie. Columbia was supportive, so we put together a track called "Business Doin' Pleasure."

It was a disaster; the song wasn't that great to begin with because Cheba definitely was not Shock G, an artist who was the full package as a writer and a performer. Then we sent the two-inch tape to Teena in L.A. at her home studio. When she went to lay her vocal down, something happened to the two-inch tape, so we had to make another copy and send it out. The problem was she billed additional costs for the studio's mistake—a studio she owned in her house. When I called her to discuss it, she yelled at me and hung up on me. This was not the first nor would it be the last time somebody tried to get one over on us. It did not matter; Joe and I came to the conclusion this whole thing was ill-conceived from the start. The fact remained: Cheba was not an artist.

Back when I started the marketing and promotion company with Jackie and Rose, I was contacted by a lot of labels looking for help with their artists. One guy named Mio Vukovic was an A&R guy at Geffen Records. He was a DJ who formed a partnership with another A&R guy named Jeff Fenster, who was formerly a lawyer for Warner Brothers Records and came to Geffen as an A&R guy. Geffen Records and its namesake founder were on top of the world. David Geffen is a legendary music business figure. He started in the mailroom at the William Morris Agency and went on to become Laura Nyro's manager. From there, his career took on a phenomenal trajectory, working with artists like Neil Young, as well as Jackson Browne, who introduced him to The Eagles. At one point, Geffen's company had the number one film, number one movie, and number one Broadway production all at the same time. Geffen Records was the premier label for rock with hit records by Guns & Roses, Aerosmith, the Black Crowes, and, soon, Nirvana.

Mio and Jeff had signed some hip-hop artists, The 7A3, a rap group produced by Lawrence "Muggs" Muggerud from L.A., and Silk Tymes Leather, a female rap group from Atlanta produced by fifteen-year-old Jermaine Dupri. At that time, Geffen was a premier rock label. It had very little black music of note. It was not within their culture as a label. Geffen Records hired me to do marketing and promotion for The 7A3 and Silk Tymes Leather, and they hired Joe to mix these records. Neither of these projects took off, but our relationship with Jermaine and his father (and manager) Michael Mauldin, as well as our relationship with Muggs, led to events that would later put Ruffhouse on the map.

Joe was in L.A. mixing a record by an artist named Mellow Man Ace called "Mentirosa," Spanish for liar. While mixing,

Mellow Man told Joe that his brother, Sen, had a rap group Joe should check out. It was called Cypress Hill—a rap duo with a DJ and percussionist. Their performances were coincidentally produced by Muggs, who was also the DJ. Mellow Man gave Joe the cassette. Joe brought the cassette back from L.A. and shared it with me. I really liked it. Around this same time, we had signed a rap artist—Larry Larr—through Chuck Nice, the DJ for a Philadelphia rap group called Three Times Dope, who had some moderate success. Larry came from the storytelling school days of rap, like Will Smith, Doug E. Fresh, Slick Rick, and others.

We were scheduled to meet with our then-A&R rep at Columbia Records, Kevin Woodley, about the Larry Larr *Da Wizard of Odds* record. Joe and I drove up to New York for the meeting, and Joe's brother, Phil, came along.

We arrived at Columbia, and to our surprise, we learned Kevin Woodley was let go from the Columbia A&R department; his replacement was Kurt Woodley (no relationship). Kurt had a very credible background. He had worked with Andre Harrell's Uptown Records and had discovered Mary J. Blige. He signed her as part of a three-girl vocal group to a management company he started in a storefront office.

On the day of our meeting, Kurt unapologetically told us he was not feeling Larry Larr. He thought the whole commercial storytelling rap style had run its course and audiences wanted a more street-oriented narrative from artists. We disagreed and ended the meeting.

But before we left, I gave Kurt a copy of the Cypress Hill tape.

That night, after we had returned to Philadelphia from the meeting at Columbia, Kurt Woodley called me. He was digging the Cypress Hill demo, and he played it for Donnie Ienner. So, we called Muggs and offered a singles deal. Muggs sent us a DAT (digital audio tape) of five new songs, which they recorded with money they received from signing with BMG publishing. Every song was better than the last. There was no doubt which record we were doing next.

CHAPTER SIX

HAND ON THE PUMP

P hiladelphia was changing. Although Philadelphia was a sizable city in terms of geography, its skyline was not very impressive compared to other cities its size, due to an archaic zoning law that once dictated no building could be higher than the statue of William Penn sitting atop city hall. This zoning law was repealed in 1986, and Philadelphia really started to grow. Almost at once, there were building projects everywhere, and a new highway—476—was built connecting 76 through the city to I-95.

Almost as if by some kind of relative reaction, Ruffhouse also started to come into its own. Kurt Woodley at Columbia sent us a tape by a hip-hop artist from the Bronx named Tim Dog, who had done tracks with the Ultramagnetic MCs. It was a very interesting answer record called "Fuck Compton," but it was not an answer record to any particular song. It was a very provocative proclamation on West Coast hip-hop culture. In the song, Tim disparaged NWA members Eazy-E and Dr. Dre, as well as commented on West Coast gang warfare with one lyric stating: "All that gang shit is for dumb muthafuckas."

This was a very dicey proposition. Tim seemed to not be worried about retribution, but I think he was smart enough to not want to find himself hanging out in the wrong parts of L.A. On top of that, a huge posse of his guys was featured in the "Fuck Compton" video, directed by Rich Murray production protégé James Brummel. James did this video for five thousand dollars, and it ended up being the first music video ever sold commercially. We sold over one hundred thousand copies of the video single for $9.99, reaching top ten on the *Billboard* Rap Singles chart. I thought Tim Dog was hoping to draw the NWA guys and other celebrated West Coast rappers into an exchange on record, but they did not take the bait. Responding only would have propelled Tim's sales and market presence.

After the hoopla of the single, we put together an album called *Penicillin on Wax*—a great record production-wise with some incredible hardcore elements. But it did not achieve the level of anticipated success we thought it would. Also, the hip-hop audience was now being more discerning. A hit single did not mean automatic album sales. Hip-hop music was now becoming an album-oriented medium, and Tim Dog could not expand his repertoire in a way that generated long play sales.

Rick Chertoff left Columbia to go to MCA, where he went on to sign Joan Osborne. His replacement as head of A&R at Columbia was David Kahne, an A&R executive from L.A. who was also a producer who had worked with Fishbone and Sugar

Ray. We were sad to see Rick leave, but we got on with David immediately. Like Rick, he was a real music guy.

Def Jam Records was a rap empire distributed by Columbia Records/CBS, with artists like LL Cool J, Public Enemy, and Onyx, among others. As a result of their success, CBS (now Sony Music as a result of Sony Corporation's purchase of the CBS Records division) became the number one distributor for hip-hop. Def Jam left Sony shortly after we came aboard. Donnie Ienner and David Kahne knew that hip-hop needed to come from an entity outside of a major label, so they were very supportive of us.

At this time, we were working on the Cypress Hill project. Our initial offer to Cypress Hill was for a twelve-inch single, which was our commitment to release one song with the option to do additional singles and album-length releases. After they had recorded the five songs with BMG, the singles deal was off the table, and we ended up committing to an album (with a budget of eighty-five thousand dollars).

Cypress Hill flew out from L.A. and spent the next few weeks finishing the record with Joe. They were laid back and were very cool guys with amiable dispositions and an incredible penchant for weed. The Cypress Hill record was like nothing out there. It had true artistry on every level. Louis "B-Real" Freese and Senen "Sen Dog" Reyes were West Coast rappers proclaiming the virtues of weed and other aspects of life on the streets.

What set them apart was their ability to present their stories from the perspective of being a product of their social microcosm. This, combined with DJ Muggs's incredible battery of funky breaks and loops and Joe's trademark bombastic mix, made the first Cypress album (simply entitled *Cypress Hill*) a masterpiece. We delivered it to Columbia and set a release date for August of 1991.

We shipped about thirty thousand albums. While the record was critically acclaimed and DJs rang our phones nonstop, we could not get real market penetration. The album sat like a stick in the mud. But this would soon change. At the same time, Jermaine Dupri, the fifteen-year-old producer of Silk Tymes Leather, was actively developing artists for his production company So So Def. His father, Michael Mauldin, was also his manager. They sent us a demo by a twelve-year-old rap duo Jermaine was producing.

They were called Kris Kross.

The two members were both named Chris. Chris Kelly and Chris Smith wore their clothes backwards, a marketing hook devised by Jermaine. Jermaine had met them in a shopping mall in Atlanta. Although they were hip-hop artists, I think a lot of people upon meeting them would forget they were also twelve-year-old kids. When it came to the business of being Kris Kross, they both were very quiet and never let their guard down, which I took as their attempt to show hip-hop attitude. But once you got them out of the role, such as when I took them out of the studio to go hang out on South Street, go shopping, or go to the movies, they would relax and become kids again. Chris Smith, a.k.a. Daddy Mac, was quiet and pensive while Chris Kelly, a.k.a. Mac Daddy, was more outspoken. I do not think they could ever have imagined what lay ahead.

We offered a singles deal. It was not that we were being cheap; it was just sound business practice to be careful with money we advanced to artists because it would get recouped against all the records we released. For example, we use monies from our distributor, Sony, to sign artist A, artist B, and artist C. We release records by all three. Artists A and B fail while artist C's record sells like hotcakes, and there are profits. Sony will recoup all monies lost on artists A and B before splitting the proceeds from the profits of artist C. This is called "cross collateralization," and it is something you need to always keep in mind when constructing deals.

Anyway, we initially agreed to a singles deal. Kris Kross's demo had a song called "Lil' Boys in da Hood." I liked this song because I thought it was unique—a twelve-year-old questioning where he wanted to go in life. Did he want to emulate the drug dealers with the money, cars, and clothes? Or did he want to go to school and do other things? It was a powerful subject matter and, as far as I knew, had never been done before. We ended up committing to a five song EP, or "Extended Play Record." The EP was made popular in the post-punk era in Europe. A new rock band could invite the audience to spend five or six dollars for five songs rather than investing eleven dollars for a long play album. This gave the audience an opportunity to make a smaller investment to get to know the artist before committing to the expensive long play full album. We thought this would be a great idea for Kris Kross, and Jermaine and Michael Mauldin agreed.

But soon enough, my idea for Kris Kross to be this kind of introspective listeners project went out the window. They did a song in the studio called "Jump." It was a noisy little track made up of layered samples containing the piano from the Jackson 5's "I Want You Back." Admittedly, I was not really into this song at first, but I understood its appeal. But I was amazed how everybody else was freaking out over it. We sent it up to David Kahne, and he suggested adding a bass line on it. Joe did this, and one night, I was leaving the Ruffhouse office when a fax came through from Michael Mauldin:

"Chris, Kris Kross 'Jump' is going to be a number one song! Michael."

I should have kept it and framed it. The anticipated excitement for the Kris Kross song soon obliterated the concept of an EP, and we did a deal for an album. But although we committed to the album, I do not think anybody could have foreseen how big this project would be.

In January of 1992, the Cypress Hill song "How I Could Just Kill a Man" ended up in the soundtrack for the movie *Juice*, starring Omar Epps and Tupac Shakur. It played in a scene where Tupac's character was chasing Omar Epps's character with a gun. As a result of this exposure, the Cypress Hill album *Cypress Hill*, which had been languishing at retail, exploded, selling fifty thousand copies a week. Things at Ruffhouse were about to get crazy.

Muggs from Cypress Hill started a production company called Soul Assassins. One of the first artists he produced was a rap group called House of Pain, featuring Everlast, a rapper who had previously made a little noise as one of the early white rappers. Muggs gave us a demo for House of Pain, but the songs were not quite developed. Cypress Hill signed a deal with a management company called Buzztone, owned by Amanda Scheer and Happy Walters. One day, Amanda called me and proceeded to tell me that, apparently, House of Pain also had a song called "Jump"—and we had stolen it to give to Kris Kross.

I could not believe the absurdity of what she was telling me. "Jump" was written and conceived in its entirety by Jermaine Dupri. I retrieved the original House of Pain demo while I was on the phone with Amanda. The demo from House of Pain did not have a song called "Jump" on it or anything remotely close. Everlast had to change the title of his song from "Jump" to "Jump Around." Amanda warned that Everlast was going to fuck Joe up.

What made the whole thing completely laughable was that

our song and their song sounded nothing alike. Amanda and Happy were, for the most part, cool, but with Amanda, there was always some kind of drama. Happy and I would chat on the phone for a good while, and suddenly Amanda would start talking, as she had been listening in the whole time without making her presence on the call known beforehand. It was very strange, as though they did not want each other to be on the phone with the label without the other hearing what was going on. As far as the song controversy went, I thought this was Amanda stoking the fire.

House of Pain's song became a huge hit, but Everlast could not let go of his beef about the songs. At the end of the video for "Jump Around," he called out Joe, referring to him as "Joe the Biter" Nicolo, a smear on Joe's handle, "Joe the Butcher."

But none of this drama could stop the juggernaut of Kris Kross's "Jump."

Rich Murray shot the video in Atlanta for twenty-one thousand dollars. As usual, Rich, in true form, delivered a video that should have cost substantially more. The video caught the Chrises' personalities and performance. The video was ready for radio, MTV, BET, and all of the video outlets. Columbia's marketing department had persuaded the actress Rosie Perez, who was the talent coordinator for the television show *In Living Color*, to book Kris Kross to perform "Jump" on the show. The single was not yet released to radio.

The morning after the performance aired, Myrna and I were at a diner on Overbrook Avenue near our apartment. I overheard an older, middle-aged couple sitting across from us talking about Kris Kross. The guy was going on about seeing them on *In Living Color* and how great these little kids were.

I looked at Myrna and said, "This record is going to be huge."

Huge was really not the word to describe the success of this song. "Tsunami" was probably closer. It was unbelievable how this group, Kris Kross—and Cypress Hill, for that matter—impacted popular American youth culture in a way none of us could have predicted. "Jump" was so big that every time I got in my car, I could find it playing on any one of three radio stations.

A national Kris Kross Day was established where all elementary school kids wore their clothes backward to school. Macy's department store put all of the clothes on their mannequins backward for this day, too. The single knocked Boys II Men's "End of the Road" (also recorded at Studio 4) off the number one spot on the *Billboard* Pop Singles chart and stayed there for eleven weeks. I was so busy and running around that, when the album came out, I was not even thinking of the charts. I walked into Ruffhouse one morning to find boxes of gourmet pizza and cases of Dom Pérignon champagne sent from Donnie Ienner. The album had shipped number one.

In March of 1992, Kris Kross's *Totally Krossed Out* album sold half a million copies a week for the first few weeks. And Ruffhouse now had a full-time staff. Rose did retail marketing, Kevin Bass, a recent Wharton grad, helped out in a general manager capacity, Jeff Coulter did all of the administration, Dave Janofsky did radio promotion, Evan Gusz did college radio, and Glenn Manko did publicity. We also had a smattering of interns, including Ahmir "Questlove" Thompson, who would go on to be the drummer for the one of the biggest, well-known hip-hop groups of all time, The Roots. At the time, they called themselves "Square Roots" and they had already established a communal following of local fans. I gave Ahmir money for the Square Roots to make a video for a song called "Pass the Popcorn". In the years to come, The Roots would become one of hip-hop's biggest artists. They, along with Jazzy Jeff's "Touch of Jazz" production company, would form the bedrock of Philadelphia's Neo-Soul movement. All this would be headquartered out of Larry Gold's recording studio, "The Studio," where producers like James Poyser plied their craft in a whole new sub-genre of music. Other producers like Dre & Vidal, and Carvin & Ivan, would also help to establish Philadelphia as the home of Neo-Soul.

Ruffhouse's one-room office was getting very cramped, so we moved down the hall to a much larger space.

During this time, I had been working overtime developing rock bands. I had previously recorded some demos for a group called Mama Volume. The songs never came to fruition. The guitar player, Bayen Butler, formed a short-lived rockabilly band called Rupert Speed. After Rupert Speed, he joined a band called Dandelion. I really liked Dandelion. They were a great band, and I kind of thought Joe maybe thought it was a folly. We did an independent album release for the band called *I Think I'm Gonna Be Sick*, which, although it did not sell well, was picked up overseas by Sony labels there.

Luc Vergier, an international marketing guy for Columbia Records who worked out of the Sony Music offices on Marlborough Street in London, and I became very good friends. Luc became a critical piece of the Ruffhouse International machinery. Luc was formally a DJ who grew up in Marseille, France, and moved to London. His wife, Donna, did international marketing for Mute Records, the same company that distributed Rhythm King. Luc really took a sense of proprietorship in all of the Ruffhouse releases. He made sure we had radio and retail coverage in every market internationally. I always considered international to be a fertile market for hip-hop. When I went to Europe with Schoolly a few years back, we did shows in front of audiences who had never seen a hip-hop artist perform live. Now, Luc was quick on the draw on both Cypress Hill and Kris Kross; we were selling records in volume numbers all over the world.

When the Dandelion record was released, Luc set up tours for them in Europe. It was important to me that this band see some success because I felt that, despite the success we were having, we needed an artist outside of hip-hop to give Ruffhouse a little more dimension as an A&R source. The band was very talented, but certain members had a very anti-record label attitude, which was in keeping with a lot of popular bands at the time. Modern rock bands were far from the day of limousines and videos shot on exotic island locations. Then, it was about beat-up Converse Chuck Taylors and thrift store sweaters. Anything that looked or smelled like the machinations of major label money was completely taboo and frowned upon in modern rock culture. Even grubby little Ruffhouse was considered, in the alternative rock world, to be a little too shiny. I thought the whole mentality was absurd; while these bands preached socialist values, they definitely wanted the major label money. An A&R executive at Columbia told me that when Green Day came to Columbia to discuss the possibility of signing with them, the band thought Columbia's offices looked too corporate, and then signed to Warner Brothers instead. I, personally, did not see what the physicality of the building had to do with the people that worked there, but this was how a lot of rock artists were thinking at that time. Dandelion was no exception. Although I found it annoying, I could not argue with their music. So, I let their anti-label banter go in one ear and out the other, and we decided to do another album together.

My father was very proud when I called him from the Times Square Marriott and told him that Cypress Hill was being shown on Sony's Times Square electronic billboard. My father was very happy with my success, and I wanted to show him some thanks for his support. At this time, he was separated from my mother and living in Strafford, Pennsylvania, the next town over from Devon. He had let me stay at his apartment rent-free a few times when I was working as a cook and starting in the music business. He worked in a mattress store and kept newspaper clippings of the frequent stories about Ruffhouse. I bought a Rolls Royce for myself, and I bought him a silver Mercedes-Benz. My father always wanted one, and I was very happy to do this.

By July of 1992, Kris Kross's album went multiplatinum, and Cypress Hill's album had well exceeded a million units. But Joe and I were too busy to soak in this success. Since the first Cypress record had been out a while before it blew up, the group was already in the preproduction phase of a new record while they were touring the first record. It was time to shake the tree at Sony for some money for the company and the album.

But before that could happen, Amanda Scheer at Buzztone called me and said Cypress was being hit with cease and desist letters from lawyers representing songwriters, publishers, and labels claiming Cypress Hill had sampled their music and did not clear it for use in their songs. There were samples taken from artists like Sly and the Family Stone, The Youngbloods, James Brown, Buju Banton, and others. This was bad news as Cypress Hill's first record was flying off the shelves. If an artist samples a piece of music, no matter if it's only a few seconds, it's considered "willful infringement," and the damages are awarded per each record manufactured and sold. It's considered the most severe violation in terms of copyright laws.

The correct way to clear a sample is this: The existing song, which the artist wants to sample, and a copy of the artist's song, containing the sampled piece, are submitted to the publisher and record company who own the original composition. They, in turn, have to approve it, with permission granted by everybody involved in the song being sampled, from the writers to the publishers and the original label. In all, this could be many people. Once everybody agrees, then the artist who samples the song is given a mechanical license for an "interpolation," which is a new composition, with the ownership split among the original writers and the new writers. When an artist puts out a record with an uncleared sample, the terms are more favorable for the original writers as they have the legal advantage.

When artists make sample requests ahead of time, there are many factors considered. The popularity of the song being sampled dictates the size of splits and advances. On the other hand, the popularity of the artist who samples a song also impacts this, as a popular artist sampling an older song breathes new life into an existing composition, giving new revenues to songwriters who would have not received it otherwise.

The cost to go back and clear the samples on the Cypress Hill record after the fact was over $500,000 dollars. Cypress's lawyers and management tried to get us to absorb the costs, but we refused, mainly because we were still in a production arrangement with Sony. Cypress, as the artist, was making the lion's share of the revenues generated from sales. Sony, as the distributor, fronted the monies out to the claimants, but they recouped it from the royalties owed to Cypress under the venture, not Ruffhouse's. There were some very notorious sample claims in the business in the years to come, some of them involving Ruffhouse artists. As a result, Sony and other majors adopted a checks-and-balances system, which meant they would not go to manufacture unless all samples were cleared.

In July of 1992, Ruffhouse went through some growing pains. Our deal with Sony for the $125,000 a year overhead was not cutting it anymore, thanks in part to the growth of the label and the success of the Ruffhouse artists.

We needed to restructure our deal with Sony. This was not something that Sony or any other major does without a bit of angst. They were not in the business of giving money away if they didn't have to. Donnie Ienner was riding on a huge wave of success. In one stealth move, he made Def Jam's departure from Columbia painless by bringing in Ruffhouse. The one thing Joe and I knew was that there was no way Def Jam would sell the amount of records Ruffhouse sold for the same profit participation we made. Fred Ehrlich was the general manager at Columbia. He was the guy we dealt with in our first renegotiation. When I pointed out the success of Kris Kross, his response was, "Why should Columbia be penalized for making a great business deal?"

"Yes, but why should Ruffhouse be penalized for signing an artist for seventy-five thousand dollars who is now making you tens of millions?" I countered.

I liked Fred a lot. He was organized, straightforward, and did not bullshit. He was about business and was very good at explaining what things cost and where the money went. The lawyers from both sides went back and forth over a period of six weeks. We finally received an amendment to our existing agreement. We received better terms.

In August, I flew over to Ireland and London to see Kris Kross, who were on tour with Michael Jackson. I took my buddy Greg McGarrah. Greg worked part-time at Ruffhouse and was the manager of a nightclub I frequented called Revival. When I met up with the Kris Kross contingency at the hotel, I was admittedly surprised at how much stardom had shrunk them into a bubble. When they were in Philadelphia making the record, I took them to restaurants and shopping, hanging out on South Street many times.

Now, we could not even go down the block to a restaurant. Every movement required military planning with security and logistics. If they wanted to go to a movie, they had to call ahead, reserve the last two rows of the theater, come in during the very beginning of the movie, and leave before the end to avoid getting mobbed. All in all, they looked tired and shell-shocked.

The venues in Dublin and London were stadiums. Kris Kross had quite an amazing stage show, but the Michael Jackson part was interesting. Before Michael went on stage, everybody needed to evacuate the entire backstage area. His people built a plywood tunnel covered in garbage bags from underneath the stage running out through the cargo loading area to the back-lot entrance. He was driven over in a van right to the tunnel entrance and came up through the stage floor. Nobody, including his own musicians, saw him until he started singing the first song. The show was spectacular, as you would expect it to be.

Everything was right with the world; I had stopped taking independent marketing and promotion gigs. Meanwhile, Joe was as busy as he could be. He was not happy I partied as much as I did, but it did not keep me from performing.

But there were other people who did try and undermine my relationship with Joe.

Andy Kravitz was one of Studio 4's mainstay musicians. He was a spectacular drummer, and I never had an issue with his talent. At first, we got along. I had on many occasions hung out with Andy at the studio late at night after everybody went home. But it seemed like there was always an issue with Andy over money. We hired a lot of musicians, but it seemed every time we hired Andy, the deal changed after the fact.

Joe always rolled over for Andy because Andy was important to what Joe was doing production-wise. But as talented as Andy was—and believe me, the guy could play drums on a serious level—I was not going to be extorted every time we hired him. Andy started whispering things in Joe's ear. At one point, he told Joe that I was a heroin addict. I do not think Joe believed it. For me at that time it was laughable, as I had yet to ever even try heroin. Andy and I would years later become friends after he moved to a house not far from mine and our wives started hanging out together. He would eventually admit to me he made this up in attempt to try and get rid of me because, as he said at the time, "I stood between him and the checkbook."

This was not the first time I had people trying to undermine me. A local entertainment attorney, with whom I was in a minor financial dispute, told Joe a friend of his "gave" me a gram of coke at a nightclub one night to make me go away. At that time, I did not know of anybody who "gave away" grams of coke, which made this absurd, but that part of the story was designed to make me look like a drug-crazed fiend. I called the attorney and asked to be introduced to this generous mystery man because I would like to get some more "free grams of coke." He acted like he did not know what I was talking about and denied saying this to Joe. When I offered to put Joe on the phone, the attorney started backpedaling, saying we needed to put our differences aside. Again, just like with Andy, the lawyer admitted it to me years later that he made it up.

There were a few times over the years when people knew I lived a certain lifestyle and tried to use it against me to further their own agenda. This is one of the prices I paid for drug abuse. The funny thing for me was they could never get the actual drug right. At the time, I was doing methamphetamine, not coke or heroin. But that did not matter, I did party a lot, and, much to my wife's chagrin, I refused to look at my problems.

In July of 1992, I received a phone call from MC Serch, one half of the hip-hop duo 3rd Bass, who had some big records on Def Jam. Serch was involved in a soundtrack for a film called *Zebrahead*, starring Michael Rapaport. The film explored the subject of race and the assimilation of hip-hop culture by white people. Serch was also working with an artist named Nas, who I was familiar with because Greg McGarrah had been going on and on about Nas for months. Greg was incessantly playing this tape by Main Source, "Live at the Barbeque," which featured Nas. I couldn't disagree, as it was undeniable that Nas had the potential to be a stand-alone artist. At the time, I was for some reason under the impression that Nas was already signed to a label called Wild Pitch, and my thoughts were that since he was already on this label, the cost would be astronomical to buy him out of his contract. So when Serch came down to Philadelphia with Nas and Faith Newman, an A&R rep for Columbia Records, I could not have been more thrilled. We had lunch at the Spaghetti Warehouse, and when meeting Nas for the first time I was surprised by how young he was given how he was already so advanced lyrically. We signed Nas to Ruffhouse. We did the soundtrack for *Zebrahead* and released the song "Halftime," which got major acclaim. James Brummel did a very cool low-budget video for it that got tons of airplay both in the States and overseas. During the production of Nas's record, John Schecter from *The Source*

magazine—one of the most popular hip-hop publications—
came down to the office to visit. He asked for a copy of Nas's
demo to preview, which I gave him. Nas's album would be the
most anticipated new artist release in the history of hip-hop.

CHAPTER SEVEN

TRICKS OF THE SHADE

At the beginning of 1993, Cypress Hill was completing their second record, *Black Sunday*, at the same time that Kris Kross was doing its second record, *The Bomb*. While we were mixing the Cypress Hill record in the studio, Donnie Ienner came down with David Kahne to listen to it. The first record was a masterpiece, and the second record gave you everything you were expecting. I felt like we were on top of the world, and there was more to come.

When it came to Philadelphia nightlife, I was the prince of the city. Restaurant and club owners let me park my Rolls Royce—or any number of cars I had been accumulating—on the sidewalk in front of their establishments. I had several vintage Jaguars, including a gun metal '69 E-Type and a '64 S-Type with wire wheels. And I bought a 1941 Harley Davidson WLA combat motorcycle. I also occasionally bought cars for employees who needed them. I bought a '64 Thunderbird for Mike Tyler, a guitar player who played on a lot of our studio recordings. It was around this time in April of 1993 that I had a "lifestyle mishap" that could have ended it all. I was with some girls who were dancers, and we went to the home of a mutual friend in Center City to meet up with some other people. The guys went out to get alcohol while the girls and I waited behind. The girls went into the bathroom and were in there for a prolonged period of time. I knocked on the door, and they opened it up to reveal they were doing heroin. I had never done anything opiate related, but was I was curious, and my confidence got the better of me. Heroin was making a comeback as a new drug of choice. I was insistent about trying it and against their better judgment, they gave me some. I snorted a line and do not remember anything but falling back into a bathtub. The girls panicked and left me there. My friends arrived back at the house as the girls were running out the door. They were unsuccessful in reviving me and called an ambulance. I recall waking up with a tube inserted in my throat and trying to pull it out. The paramedics were cursing at me. They took me to Jefferson Hospital, where I had been born. It was probably the most frightening situation I had ever been in. Not to mention embarrassing. You would have thought this event would serve as a deterrent for things that would happen years later, too, but I wasn't that smart.

That spring, I met Bobby DeDomenico and Tommy Connelly, who owned a restaurant on South Street, Philadelphia, called Lickety Split. I got to know Bobby particularly well because I used to frequent Lickety Split quite often. They showed me a space on the second floor of a building up the street from Lickety Split. They told me they wanted to open a night club there and fashion it after the Monte Carlo Living Room, an upscale place down the street at Second and South. They needed investors. I discussed with Joe about the prospect of investing with them. We decided to collectively invest a hundred and fifty thousand dollars. The club would be called Club Niccolae's.

Renovations began. When everything was done, the decorating (which we had nothing to do with) turned out to be substandard. Chrome railings and framed Nagel prints, like something you see in an airport bar, were installed. Our contribution in that regard was to put in a state-of-the-art sound system. All was set to go.

On opening night, we started to play music, and around 10:00 p.m., the first issue occurred. Our club was situated on the second floor above Tower Books, which, like their music retail counterpart, Tower Records, was open until midnight. The music was barely on for five minutes when Tower Books's employees came up to complain. Great, we just opened up a nightclub above a bookstore, open seven nights a week until 12 a.m. This was brilliant planning! Even I did not anticipate this problem.

But this was only the beginning of the problems. The place never made money. Only the police and the Pennsylvania Liquor Board were frequent visitors. The club was renamed "Nicole's" in an attempt to cater to the younger crowd. Eventually, when that didn't work, it was renamed "Nicky's" and turned into a go-go bar. It was pathetic. In retrospect, I am not even sure why we took on that venture, except maybe out of ego. Why did we give a shit about owning a nightclub? It did not fit in with our core business model.

About this time, a local music attorney named Kevon Glickman brought in a Philadelphia hip-hop group called the Goats, who were backed up by a full band. We ended up signing them. The three main members were Oatie Kato, Madd, and Swayzac. The first album, *Tricks of the Shade*, was called "political hip-hop satire" by music journalists. We did a video for the song "Typical American" with Rich Murray. By now, Rich had been doing videos for a lot of important artists, including the Spin Doctors, which launched Rich into the upper stratosphere of music video directors. The Goats were well received at college radio, but more importantly, their record was picked up internationally, even though they had not yet sold many records in the States. As with all Ruffhouse releases, London-based Luc Vergier was very good at making sure we had international coverage with DJs and journalists, who all found the Goats to be a refreshing new voice in hip-hop.

The Goats' manager, Kevon Glickman, was a music attorney who grew up in Villanova. He moved to New York, where he met his wife, Susan, and subsequently relocated back to Philadelphia. Kevon was a brilliant attorney who could have pursued other opportunities in law, but he chose music. We became good friends, and as a result of our relationship, he became instrumental later on in Ruffhouse's future.

ACCUMULATING AND MAINTAINING good friendships and working relationships came easy, but maintaining family relationships was a whole other story. I mostly avoided family gatherings, even years after my childhood abuse. I certainly did not keep in touch with many of them. I think most of my family would never have known I was married had my youngest sister Beth not come to the ceremony.

John was living in California, and Kevin and George lived in Maryland where they married and started families. They had eyes on their futures and willingly swept the ugliness of their past under the rug. At family functions like weddings, funerals, and family reunions, they acted as though nothing ever happened at the house in Devon. They all stood around and smiled, as though we were some kind of normal family. I found myself surprisingly restrained and would just mask my anxiety with alcohol. I spent every waking hour since leaving that house in Devon trying to assimilate to normal life. But my childhood still haunted me in my sleep. I often woke up at 3:00 a.m. screaming in my sleep and terrifying Myrna. My drug and alcohol use helped dull the edges and mask the anger. I started using cocaine frequently, as now I could afford it.

But there is always a breaking point. I was in London with Myrna and had been out partying with a bunch of people in the record business. I got back to the hotel that night, and Myrna was pissed. After I went to sleep, she booked a flight and flew back to Philadelphia without me. Upon returning, Myrna threw down the gauntlet, and I went off to rehab in Valley Forge. I spent a day in detox, followed by counseling and group therapy. When I hung out with the other patients—who were all there for heroin—they asked me, as the new patient, what I was there for.

"Cocaine," I replied. They said coke was easy to get off, but dope was much harder. After about four to five days, I started to believe them.

"I don't need to be here, I feel fine," I thought. The facility allowed me to go on a DMA (Discharged against Medical Advice). Like everything else, leaving rehab prematurely was not smart, and I knew it. But I knew if I stayed around, I would have to look at myself and my past; I did not know if I could do it. It was the first of many golden opportunities to have a chance to heal after my family sent me into the world as a shattered human being. It was just straight-up cowardice for me to just move on and forget. I toned down my drinking and forwent cocaine for a good while.

After getting home, I decided maybe it was time I moved out of the city. Myrna and I found a house in Wayne, Pennsylvania, not far from where I grew up. It was a nice split-level house, secluded on a hill at the end of a cul-de-sac. I enlisted the help of two Ruffhouse employees, Evan Gusz and Glenn Manko, to move in the midst of a snowstorm. We loaded up the contents of our old apartment into a fifteen-foot box truck. We drove to the new house, but I could not get the truck up the steep driveway.

The prospect of trying to move the cargo by hand up the driveway in a snowstorm was not very favorable. I dumped bags of salt up and down the length of the driveway and backed the truck up to the end of the road. My thought was that the truck would either make it up the driveway or end up in front of the lower part of the property. I drove the truck down the street at a fast clip, and it went all the way up the driveway. I laid my head on the wheel thinking that was a stupid thing to do, but it worked.

The new Cypress Hill and Kris Kross albums came out, making Joe and me millionaires. Ruffhouse was on top. I was now driving into the city every day. Frankly, the commute sucked. Joe and Phil had been doing it for years, and I-76 was getting worse by the day.

Things at the studio had not been going well between Dave Johnson and the Nicolo brothers. Lately, Phil was coming into his own as a rock producer. Dave, who always managed the studio, felt that his position as a studio manager hindered him from being able to develop his skills as a producer. Dave was not without ability. He did eventually produce G. Love and Special Sauce as well as a Ben Folds Five record, but he did not have the same intuitive production abilities that Joe and Phil had.

Back in our first year working together, when Joe and I were still calling Ruffhouse Pyramid Productions, we entered into a spec agreement with the studio. Spec or "speculation agreements" are commonplace contractual mechanisms where a recording studio will record an artist or band for free—"speculatively"—with the idea being that, if the artist or band gets signed, the studio will get percentage points on the project. After the success of the Kris Kross project, Dave felt he should be getting royalties on the Kris Kross and Cypress Hill records. The problem was that the Kris Kross and Cypress Hill records were not recorded on spec; they were paid for by Ruffhouse. Dave was constantly trying to corner me to get me to agree to sign some document or another, but it was never going to happen.

Other drama involved, unsurprisingly, Andy Kravitz, who had a studio project with a singer that was actually quite good. We played it for Columbia, and they liked it, so we decided to do an album. When we negotiated the deal, the project was represented by a local music attorney, Brad Rubens. I don't remember how, but Dave Johnson's then-girlfriend, Clare Godholm, a music attorney, negotiated on Ruffhouse's behalf. Brad told Clare they wanted a two-album deal. Two-album deals are extremely rare and are only done in circumstances where the artist is the subject of a bidding war among the labels. Two-album deals call for the label to commit to doing two albums upfront. In other words, instead of doing one album and having an option to do more based on the performance of the first album, the label is obligated to do two albums regardless of the performance of the first release. On top of that, most two-album deals include the label advancing money for the second record at the same time they give the artist or band the initial advance.

I was traveling when Brad asked Clare for this. Instead of saying no, which should have been a suitable response, Clare went to Joe who said yes. I do not think Joe understood what she was asking him. As if that was not enough, Sony would have to approve that deal, and there was no way in hell they or anybody, for that matter, should.

So, I said no, plain and simple.

After production started on the first album, Andy incorrectly decided one day, after reading the agreement, that we were somehow obligated to give him additional monies. So, educating Andy on that was another needless serving of shit. The cherry on top that sunk the ship was that Sony wanted to see the artist perform live at a showcase at Sony Studios so they could ascertain what they were going to market. Andy refused to do the performance unless we paid him additional monies. I decided, at that point, enough was enough. It was time to cut this project loose.

Joe decided it was my fault, due to my "adversarial relationship" with Andy. I never had an argument with Andy's talent or with the music, but Andy could act completely irrational, and Joe knew that. I did not care; I was not going to jeopardize Ruffhouse's standing with Sony by bringing in a disaster-prone project. Who knows what mischief Andy would start once the record was scheduled for release? In addition to that, this was a studio project that would have required a full-time salaried band. Who was going to pay for that on top of the cost of making the record? Not Ruffhouse and certainly not Sony. I was not going to be extorted anymore. The project died on the vine.

The problem with making money is that, when you become successful, everybody tries to rob you night and day. A guy named Bilal brought us an artist called C.E.B. (Countin' Endless Bank), who we then signed. C.E.B. was made up of Cool C and Steady B from the Hilltop Hustlers. Steady B was a relation to Lawrence and Dana Goodman, the owners of Pop Art Records who put out the Jazzy Jeff and Fresh Prince records through Jive. Lawrence and Dana were out of the music business picture at that point.

We started out with a single called "Get the Point," which reached number five on the Hot Rap singles chart in *Billboard*. This success, I think, was equally due to the well-oiled Ruffhouse/Sony marketing and promotion machine. But Bilal was just another in a long line of "cell phone managers"—people with limited experience in the business. Now, this is not to say that you need to be experienced to manage a recording artist, but you cannot rewrite the principles of business to suit your situation.

Although I believed Bilal had the best of intentions, his management style left little to be desired. He showed up to the label with a handwritten receipt from City Blue, a clothing chain. The receipt was for thousands of dollars for clothing he said he bought for C.E.B., and he wanted us to reimburse him. But it does not work like that. We did not ask him to go and buy these clothes for the artist. We had clothing budgets for videos, special events, touring, and television, but these had to be approved beforehand with mechanisms to ensure checks and balances. Management is not empowered to just go out and spend money on the artist and expect the label to reimburse them. But this is a commonplace assumption where a recording agreement with a label is perceived as an opportunity for management to extort money from the label.

Some financial disputes have led to me being threatened with physical violence on many occasions. But my reply is always the same:

"I do not control the checkbook for that; you need to talk with Sony."

In the early days of the label, a group of gangsters told me that Ruffhouse needed to pay "street tax." For those not familiar with the term, street tax is money paid from one criminal to another for the privilege of conducting an illegal activity. It's a tribute, "a tax" that Ruffhouse was asked to pay as an enterprise conducting hip-hop business in Philadelphia.

Again, my reply was, "Go up to the Sony building in New York and explain it to them and see how far it gets you."

Once, Bilal wanted us to give him a management percentage of a remix budget because a lawyer had explained to him that any advance was commissionable. In theory, yes, but not production budgets. Again, my reply was no.

C.E.B.'s album was an utter failure, and the members ended up robbing a bank. A female Philadelphia police officer was killed in the attempt, the first Philadelphia female officer killed in the line of duty. Steady B got a life sentence and Cool C was sentenced to death by lethal injection.

In October of 1993, Cypress Hill was booked to perform on *Saturday Night Live*. Myrna and I went up for the live broadcast. The guest host was Vince Vaughn. At the end of their musical performance, Cypress Hill lit up a joint on live TV, causing a major blowup between *Saturday Night Live's* talent coordinator and the Columbia Records publicity department. But their penchant for weed did present a niche publicity angle. Rose was able to get Cypress Hill on the cover of *High Times* magazine, which was a big boon for the group. I did not smoke weed due to the fact that I discovered it made me think too much about everything. I would start to see plots within plots. Cypress Hill was in Philly doing a radio interview on *Power 99*. Before we went over, I smoked some weed with them at the hotel. I immediately regretted it. I was so high I could not even imagine going into the radio station.

The Goats' record, *Tricks of the Shade*, started to make some real noise. Journalists loved them, and they were touring overseas constantly. We got them on a tour opening up for a group called Big Chief. I went to a few shows, and it was apparent that after the Goats played, the crowd thinned out before Big Chief took the stage. Halfway through the tour, I got a call from Michele Anthony, an executive vice president of Sony Music. Michele was not alone on the call; an executive named Missy Worth was yelling at me about how the Goats would do their set and then go off to smoke pot, leaving their equipment on stage so the crowd would not want to wait for Big Chief to take the stage.

I said this was not the case, but she insisted that Big Chief's manager, who was a friend of hers, would never lie to her. Well, I was at the shows, and the Goats had a road crew who moved the equipment in a timely fashion immediately after the Goats performed. The fact was that just about everybody who was coming to these shows was there to see the Goats. The best thing for Big Chief was to just take the opening slot so they could get the exposure.

I liked Missy, but what bothered me was that she, a Sony executive, was taking the side of an artist who was not even on Sony and disparaging the Goats when she did not have the facts. The Goats were a hybrid rap/rock group, and Donnie Ienner liked them, as well as the Sony department heads. This was a rare occurrence where a developing artist had not only the support of the distributor but also had support of the international label. The Goats were in a prime position to really blow up.

Schoolly D had previously done some albums with Jive that had not met their expectations and then, in early 1994, completed an album for Capitol Records. Schoolly had a predominately white following, but Jive had said from the very beginning they wanted Schoolly to broaden his appeal to the black audience, and it did not work. After the album with Capitol, he was a free agent. So it made perfect sense for him to do a record for Ruffhouse.

The album was called *Welcome to America*, and the single was called "Another Sign." I thought it was one of the best things Schoolly had done since "PSK" and "Gucci Time." The song was a commentary, with a really hooky guitar lick played by Mike Tyler. Rich Murray had done the video, which was once again awesome.

We were preparing for the Nas record release when Rose came into my office to tell me that Columbia Records said it was coming out on Columbia. Serch called me and was salty about the *Zebrahead* soundtrack and said I had left him "twisting in the wind," but we did everything we could to help with its success. Unfortunately, the movie was a commercial failure at the box office. Ruffhouse cannot be blamed for that.

In a meeting with Donnie, Joe and I learned he was in hot water with Tommy Mottola for Nas not being on Columbia proper. Technically, Nas was the first—and only—artist Donnie had ever brought to us, introducing Serch to me. But that introduction was made because Columbia did not want to sign Nas initially; their mindset was that if he was on Ruffhouse, Columbia would be assuming only half the financial risk. If

Age six, my first Holy Communion

Reading *DownBeat Magazine* while on watch duty

Virtue Studios, 1618 North Broad Street, Philadelphia

Performing with Jeff Coulter at WXPN event in Philadelphia, 1982

Jesse "Schoolly D" Weaver, Parkside Avenue, Philadelphia

In the studio with
Norman Jones and Mia
"Mac Money" Evans

First video for Ruffhouse: Cheba, "The Piper," Columbia Records.
L to R: Dave Waterson, cameraman; Lenny Grodin, video producer;
Gina Harrell, video producer; Cheba; Rose Mann, Ruffhouse;
Rich Murray, director; Chris Schwartz.

Larry Larr, "Larry, That's What They Call Me" video shoot. Bottom L to R: DJ Mad Ice; Lenny Grodin, video producer; Larry Larr; Rich Murray, director; unknown; Damian Smith, manager; Chris Schwartz.

With Myrna on
penthouse balcony
overlooking
Philadelphia, 1990

Courtesy of the author

Courtesy of the author

With my daughter, Ava, playing with one of our baby goats

Kriss Kross: Mac Daddy and Daddy Mac, Ruffhouse press photo

Kris Kross video shoot. L to R: Joe Nicolo, Ruffhouse; Marion Bradley, Columbia Records; Chris Schwartz; unknown production assistant; Rich Murray, director; Bart Phillips, So So Def Records.

Sen Dog, Muggs, and B-Real of Cypress Hill, Ruffhouse press photo

B-Real and Sen
Dog of Cypress Hill,
album photoshoot

Courtesy of Sony Music Photo Archives

The Goats, Ruffhouse press photo

Courtesy of Kevon Glickman

Signing EDM artist Armand Van Helden to Ruffhouse. L to R:
Joe Nicolo, Kevon Glickman, Armand Van Helden,
Neil Petricone (Armand's manager), and Chris Schwartz

Pras, Ms. Lauryn
Hill, and Wyclef from
Fugees photoshoot
for *Blunted on Reality*

Fugees performing in Haiti

Ms. Lauryn Hill during Fugees performance in Haiti

Ms. Lauryn Hill,
photoshoot for
*The Miseducation
of Lauryn Hill*

The Miseducation of Lauryn Hill album artwork

Ruffhouse crew, Grammys 1999. L to R: Myrna Schwartz,
Kevon Glickman, Rob Dippold, Kurt Woodley, Chris Schwartz,
Todd Wolfe, Luc Vergier, Rich Murray, and Angela Thomas.

Wyclef performing at NARAS Governor's Award presentation

Receiving NARAS
Governor's Award

"Outs in ya area." Bottom L to R: Young Zee, Yah Yah, Pacewon, Axe, Denzy, D.U., Nawshis, Az Izz; with Chris Schwartz (center) and Rich Murray (bottom center).

In San Francisco for Ms. Lauryn Hill's show. L to R: Rich Murray, Ruffhouse Films; Ricky Leigh Mensch, Hitz Magazine; Ronny Dove, KMEL Mix Show DJ; Chris Schwartz; Latin Prince, Hitz Magazine.

With Joe Nicolo uncovering Walk of Fame Plaque on Broad Street sidewalk, Philadelphia

Philadelphia Music Alliance Walk of Fame Award Plaque, Broad Street, Philadelphia

With "The Butcher Brothers," Phil and Joe Nicolo, at the Philadelphia Music Alliance Walk of Fame Award ceremony

With Phil Nicolo and Jesse "Schoolly D" Weaver in the studio, mixing

the project failed, they could recoup all of it from Ruffhouse's pipeline revenues. But now there was huge anticipation for Nas's album, and Columbia's strategy had backfired.

Nas's first single was "Halftime." It reached number eight on the Rap Singles chart and number twenty-five on the R&B chart for a soundtrack nobody really cared about. But the talk in the hip-hop community about Nas far exceeded any awareness created from the single and soundtrack release. Faith Newman conceded to me it was about Columbia Records needing a hip-hop success of their own. Columbia didn't want their hip-hop roster to be made up entirely of Ruffhouse artists, nor did they want to create another situation like when Def Jam left and cost them a huge revenue source. It was not out of the realm of possibility that something similar could one day happen with Ruffhouse. Sony offered to buy out Ruffhouse's interest for a sizable sum. Joe and I, as a favor to Don Ienner, and nobody else, agreed. We felt that we owed much of Ruffhouse's success to Donnie, and this was the least we could do. But it was a little hard to swallow.

Around this time, The Roots began making quite a bit of noise. The drummer, Ahmir "Questlove" Thompson, had interned at Ruffhouse. He eventually became the figurehead and most recognizable member of the group, achieving worldwide fame. I saw Ahmir constantly in those days, either on the train or at the airport.

Before The Roots were signed to Geffen Records, they had ardent fans among the Ruffhouse employees and interns. I went to see them perform at the Theatre of Living Arts.

While nobody could predict the future, my feelings about The Roots at the time were that they presented some challenges. First, they were primarily a live act. I used to look at artists like Fishbone, who toured constantly selling out medium-size venues, but did not really sell records. The Roots, at the time, were more about their live performance and their main appeal was to the alternative hip-hop audience, which was a narrow segment in those days. By this point, I felt I had a good idea of what the Ruffhouse-Sony machine could do best. Sony wanted hit singles. I think The Roots signing with Ruffhouse would have been challenging, but not unworkable. But there was a huge obstacle. We had just signed a group that was very similar to The Roots in some respects. Like The Roots, this group—the Fugees—would go on to make hip-hop music history.

CHAPTER EIGHT

FU-GEE-LA

"How does an artist get signed to a label?" There is no prescribed methodology. Record companies have A&R (Artist & Repertoire) representatives. A&R representatives are the designated people who identify talent (Artist) and oversee the production of recorded music (Repertoire). There are also "A&R scouts," a designation that was popular in the '60s and '70s and referred to regional reps hired to scout talent within their designated localities. Usually, these were not full-time jobs, and scouts were often DJs, club owners, retailers, or anybody a record company felt had their finger on the pulse in their area.

Most people believe that a demo tape has to make its way to

the head of a label before it can get any attention. This is partially true as most major labels often require the label heads
to sign off on anything above a development deal. A development deal is when a label signs an artist to a contract calling
for the artist to record a number of songs at the label's expense, after which the label has the option to enter into a
full-on recording agreement, should the demos show promise.
Independent labels are privately owned, and the owner, who is
usually also the head of A&R, definitely makes the final decision on any type of signing, be it a demo deal or album contract. Major labels are more committee-oriented; the A&R
function is spread out across layers: A&R associates, A&R directors, VP of A&R, Senior VPs, and so on.

Most major labels need the president to sign off on signings
requiring budgets over a certain amount of money; this is also
the same for video budgets, marketing monies, promotion
budgets, and other initiatives requiring significant expenditures. This is typical of any business to ensure the profit,
growth, and economic stability of the company. The overall
budgets for the fiscal year are determined by historical data
and are approved by the governing board. Budgets are tightly
controlled by accounting and play into the day-to-day decision-making for everything, including departmental heads,
business affairs, legal, and corporate affairs. Even with this
complex corporate construct, money still gets lost due to simple human nature.

What amazed me was how a rock band could become the
subject of a major label bidding war based on the thinnest of
pretenses. For example, a band may have never done a live
show, but because it was represented by this particular manager or lawyer, or because this particular label gave them an
offer, every record company started waving blank checks at the

band because nobody wanted to be left out. The mentality of "because this label wants it, then it must know something we don't, so don't let us miss out" was always absurd to me. Major labels can be like lemmings. They all follow each other over the cliff. Thus, when the artist in question does sign for the huge six- or seven-figure deal, then the pressure put on the project is immense. There is nothing organic or natural about this A&R process.

An artist can get signed to a label from outside the company A&R structure. For example, a mailroom employee has just as good of a chance of getting an artist signed to the label as any A&R rep. The key is understanding how to navigate the system to catch the ear of the right person at the right time. More often than not, the genesis of many major artists usually originates from the most unlikely of circumstances. As I always said, "Be most expecting when you are least expecting."

I was least expecting the Fugees.

In order for Ruffhouse to keep selling records, we were listening to tons of material. I was working hard to try to keep my addictions at bay. I constantly reasoned with myself that I did not have time to take care of my problems as I put the company first. Looking back, I have to admit it was a handy excuse at that time, as most addicts are not usually running successful multi-million-dollar companies in an incredibly competitive market. I did not have the time to deal with my personal problems.

Rose Mann had been bugging me for three or four months about a tape from a group from New Jersey. She received the tape from a guy named Hassan Sharif, an actor who appeared in a few TV commercials and did some stuff in music, as well. One morning, I listened to the tape in my car on the way to work. I initially thought the group was Jamaican, and the music had some interesting elements to it. The group was called the Rap Tranzlators. In the summer of 1993, Joe and I went to their manager's office located in an Upper East Side townhouse.

But this was an audition I will always remember.

Wyclef had an acoustic guitar accompanied by the large cassette player beatbox radio, which, for me, was a welcome change. I had become very bored of hip-hop groups as of late, not due to their records, but more so their live performance because their performances had become very pedestrian. It was always the same configuration: a DJ and two or more rappers. The Rap Tranzlators were a whole new gig. At that point, guitars in hip-hop were a novelty like Beastie Boys, Anthrax and Public Enemy, and Run-DMC and Aerosmith. These examples were electric guitars in a rock 'n' roll context, but for the Rap Tranzlators this was an acoustic guitar, a more organic component rather than a rock affectation.

Performance-wise, they were all over the place. It was interesting especially when, throughout their set, Clef took his clothes off and ended up performing in his boxers. It was a frenzied yet entertaining mess. I loved it, and I thought Joe did, as well, because he kept elbowing me while they did their thing. At the end of the performance though, Joe said in a very flat, matter-of-fact voice, "I don't like it..." Everybody fell into silence for a very uncomfortable twenty seconds. Then Joe exclaimed, "I love it!" We said we wanted to do a record. They were incredibly overjoyed.

I found out much later they had auditioned for every single major and independent label and were passed on by all of them by the time they got to us. Their manager was David Sonenberg, a Harvard Law graduate who managed Meatloaf as well as producer Jim Steinman. We worked out an album deal, which had a budget of $125,000. This, in contrast to what most rock artists were getting, was nothing at that time. A typical first-time signing for a rock artist was $300–400,000, mainly because it was always thought that it was more expensive to make a rock or pop-oriented record. After production started, all of my communication was with David Sonenberg and Wyclef.

When we went to get the names of the group members to designate them as contracting parties on the contract, there were only three names given, but I seem to remember at least six or seven people at the audition. We could not use the name the Rap Tranzlators because there was a rock group called Tranzlator, who, although defunct, were actually considering getting back together. So, the name was changed to the Refugees, then later shortened to the Fugees.

The Fugees were hard at work on their album. But when they delivered the first nine songs, I was somewhat disappointed that a lot of the tracks featured Pras dominating the songs. It's not that I wasn't digging Pras, but his rap style was not strong enough to my ears to carry these songs. I called David and voiced my concern, and he told me that Pras was Wyclef's cousin, and there was not much we could do about it. David suggested we get Wyclef on the phone, but I did not relish the idea of having to tell Clef that I wasn't feeling his cousin being the dominant rapper on those particular tracks. As it turned out, it was a very pleasant call, with Clef basically saying, "Don't worry, I got you."

Days later, I got a new tape, which was more in keeping with what I expected. Pras's rap, rather than dominating, instead gave the tracks a very tasty flavor. Overall, the album was refreshing, innovative, and completely different from everything out there. I loved "Vocab"; it was my favorite track on the entire record. A very young Ms. Lauryn Hill was already being talked about as a bubbling under superstar thanks to her performance in the Whoopi Goldberg film *Sister Act 2*. We scheduled the album for release in February of 1994, calling it *Blunted on Reality*. The first single was called "Boof Baf."

I was not clear on how we came up with the decision for that as the first single, but we as a label were comfortable at that point in not worrying about the commercial performance of the first single release. We definitely saw this group as a "career artist," if there was such a thing in hip-hop at that time. We scheduled the first video shoot to be done on Governors Island in New York. Rich Murray was the director, so I expected greatness. But it was a disaster. Rich would say the group kept changing the concept throughout the shoot, but I was also particularly unhappy with the overall look, which was this grainy black-and-white look. Despite the video, we moved forward with getting the Fugees some exposure.

Luc Vergier was all over the Fugees from day one. He ensured we got maximum exposure in all of the major international markets. Although the first album did not become a commercial success, the relentless touring, both domestically and overseas, caused the record to still sell six hundred to eight hundred copies a week even two years into the project. The Fugees were gaining new fans every week.

Things were happening for Dandelion, although things were rough from the start. The band was made up of two brothers, Kevin and Michael Morpurgo, as well as Carl Hinds, Bayen Butler, and Dante Cimino. We put out their first album, *I Think I'm Gonna Be Sick*, independently, and it sold about 25,000 copies, which was respectable for an independent alternative rock release. Dandelion had a great live show, had experience touring, and had enough press reviews, which made me think they were ready for a release through the Sony distribution.

We distributed the first record through RED (Relativity Entertainment Distribution). Relativity started out as a distributor mainly for heavy metal rock groups and became one of the largest independent distributors for independent labels. RED was acquired by Sony Music as part of an initiative undertaken by the majors to have their own independent distribution mechanisms. This is to help break artists independently before putting them through major distribution, particularly in the alternative rock genre where the core fan base is more easily accessed via indie record stores and touring. It is an economical way to help an artist build a constituency of fans without having to spend a huge six-figure marketing budget.

When we exercised the option for the second record, we tried to figure out who would produce it. Joe recommended Andy Kravitz. I actually thought Andy Kravitz was a good nominee, as I had no issues at all with his talent and capabilities. We tried having him do one song, but it did not turn out too well. He showed no real interest in listening to the band. He said, "That's as good as it's going to get," too many times during the session to inspire the band to want to put their record in his hands.

The album ended up being produced by Don Fleming, a producer who had previously worked with Sonic Youth. The first single was called "Weird Out," a really catchy song that got immediate radio airplay. The single charted on the *Billboard* Modern Rock chart, and the band was getting called for radio dates. All was looking good, especially when their album, *Dyslexicon*, sold 7,000 copies over the counter in the first week. The record was picked up by the Sony labels overseas, and Luc, as always, made sure we had the coverage we needed. Dandelion was booked to tour in Europe as the opening act for Don Fleming's band, Gumball.

Myrna and I went over to Europe for the tour. We started in Amsterdam. In Germany, Myrna slipped in the hotel bathroom and cut her hand on broken glass. We rushed to a hospital where two young German doctors fixed it. The hospital bill totaled $47. The tour was awesome, and the band had fans everywhere they played. I thought we were building something special, and I was excited to be breaking an act outside of hip-hop.

When we got back to the States after the tour ended, I went up to New York for a meeting at Sony. John LeShay, a marketing executive at Sony, told me there was a lot of excitement about both Dandelion and the Goats at the company. John had played the video for "Weird Out" in a label meeting with Donnie and everybody applauded. The video, which was done by the director who had done Beck's "Loser" video, was shot in a house with a bunch of strange people, and as the band wanted, it was a non-video video. But we had to edit the very end of the song in order for the video to work, and the band was very pissed off about it.

We had them booked to do a show in Chicago that was sponsored by a modern rock station there that had "Weird Out" in heavy rotation. I bought them a school bus with my personal money, so we did not have to rent vans for their live shows. They left late for the Chicago show and showed up at the show very late. The station had to move the lineup around for the show as Dandelion barely made it. When the program director told them what they had to do to accommodate Dandelion, Kevin, ever the anti-label guy, told the program director, "You are lucky we are even here." This got back to Columbia's radio promo department.

"The problem with Dandelion," as was explained to me by Jerry Blair, Columbia's Head of Radio, was that half of the modern rock programmers liked the band while the other thought they were "put together," meaning they were not a real band with a live following. This was a challenge. Radio, no matter what genre, works like this: Songs played on the radio are picked by program directors, who make their decisions based on a number of variables, with the most obvious being that the song needs to be amazing and fit the format. Most stations have research departments that monitor everything going on with the song, such as sales, video airplay, artist touring, and other indicators. They give priority to established artists who are current and have a fan base. One of their biggest tools in creating playlists is weekly conference calls with other program directors in different markets. They confer with each other to see how songs are performing in their respective markets. They discuss audience reaction—call-in requests and record sales in their markets—as reported in SoundScan. Philadelphia, for instance, is considered a very hard market in which to break rock and pop. So, if a rock band is performing well in Philadelphia, then it's a good bet it would work in other markets, as well. These program directors rely on each other as they are in separate markets and do not compete for listeners. So, when enough program directors don't like a band, it can spell disaster. Dandelion was on the tipping point.

When Dandelion's single debuted on the charts, *Billboard* interviewed Kevin. Kevin told the writer, "We don't even like this song; it was the record company's idea to put it out." This, too, did not go well with Columbia's radio department. The band wrote the song and recorded it, but it seemed, no matter what, that they wanted to sabotage their own careers.

The straw that broke the camel's back was when they were

invited up to Rhode Island to do another show sponsored by a radio station. Kevin and his brother, Mike, went to the station for an on-air interview before the show. During the interview, Kevin basically rolled his eyes whenever the DJ asked him a question and made it painfully clear that he thought the interview was a waste of his time. The station was so offended and pissed off that they not only didn't attend the show that night but they also called Columbia and went on a tirade about it. The station also talked about them on the weekly conference call with the other program directors. This was pretty much it for Dandelion; they lost all the support they had in radio, and Columbia just washed their hands of them. I could not believe an artist could come so close to success and flush it all down the toilet.

By the end of 1994, the offices at Ruffhouse were not big enough for all of the activity of the label, and Studio 4 needed to expand. We had created our own mastering facility, called Mastervoice, so we could master our own records. We also bought a fully automated SSL console for the B Room. We needed more room, which prompted us to start looking for a building. The one thing we all agreed on was the need to move out of the city. Philadelphia's payroll taxes and business taxes were less than desirable, and we were paying rent rather than building equity.

We looked at a lot of different buildings. One building that caught our eye was in nearby Manayunk. It was a turn-of-the-century multipurpose structure at the end of Main Street, and it came with its own parking. I think we ruled it out due to geographical location. Although it was technically outside of Philadelphia, it was a little hard to get to for people traveling from New York, which was a big consideration. We finally found a building in Conshohocken, a town on the upswing located about twenty minutes outside the city. It would cut Joe and Phil's driving time in half, and I was one exit away in Wayne. Built in 1900, the building was almost 40,000 square feet. It was two floors with a full basement that at one time housed a bowling alley. It was originally an "Odd Fellows" hall. The Odd Fellows was a social group, like the Masons, which, in the turn of the century, was very popular. Besides its original function as a meeting hall on the second floor, the building had been used for shops, dress manufacturing, and, at one point, a Bell Telephone Company of Pennsylvania telephone switching office.

We gutted the building ourselves, tearing out all the walls and creating two empty spaces on the first and second floors. We then used blue painter's tape to mark where we would build the studios and offices. We did not hire architects, and we were not too concerned in how we mapped out the floor-plan, except to make it functional. I found the process enjoyable, but we needed to get this done as quickly as possible. We replaced all the huge eight-foot windows on the second floor, which we needed a cherry picker lift truck to install. Air conditioning was also a big concern, as studios full of electronics and computers needed to be kept cool. We had to get a crane to put the AC units on the roof.

We built five studios, as well as the mastering lab. The Ruffhouse offices were located on the first floor at the front of the building, and we put production studios and the Studio 4 office in the back half. On the second floor, we built the A Room, with a huge live room the size of a gymnasium. We added a skylight in the middle of the ceiling. Joe built his studio, which he called his "treehouse," on the second-floor front, and my office was next to it with a smaller office in the middle. Ruffhouse had a reception area, and everybody had an office built around a conference area. It was exactly what we needed: centralized, functional, and comfortable. But, most importantly, we owned it. We also bought a used limousine and hired a driver named Chuck Erhman. Chuck was an older middle-aged guy who was a jack of all trades; he was a fantastic cook, carpenter, and handy man.

Life at Ruffhouse moved on. Kevon Glickman, the manager of the Goats, had a partnership with Radio Woodstock, a radio station in upstate New York started by one of his fraternity brothers. There was a new, reimagined version of the famous Woodstock concert being planned, and Cypress Hill was booked to perform. Through Kevon's relationship with Radio Woodstock, he was able to get the Goats booked as the opening act. This was a huge deal as the Goats were still a somewhat new artist and every other act booked on Woodstock was a big marquee name artist. Myrna and I decided we would go up to the festival with other Ruffhouse employees, like Evan Gusz, Glenn Manko, Rob Dippold, Tamara Feldman, Rich Murray, and Jeff Wells, our new general manager. We also had a head of regional street team promotion, Robert "Big Bob" Crippen. This group, along with Rose Mann and Jeff Coulter, were, under Joe and me, the core people responsible for the day-to-day operation of the label. I got to know Kevon very well, and we soon brought him on as our head of business affairs. We were now completely self-sufficient. We did not need outside legal counsel, except when we did major renegotiations. We rented some cars and a van and drove to the Woodstock festival.

There were a few hiccups with the Woodstock concert planning. One problem was that the guitar player for the Goats also played in another band and had a gig scheduled at the same time as Woodstock. He did not want to miss this gig, so he said he would not be available for the show. I didn't understand this. When you are in a band signed to a label, why would you prioritize doing a side project performance—in a coffee house, nonetheless—over an important show like this? To fix the situation, we enlisted Ian Cross, a fantastic guitar player and producer to step in, learn the songs, and do the show. I had met Ian years earlier when we'd cross paths in the local Philly music scene while in our respective bands (me, Tangent; he, Bricklin). Ian's band went on to secure a record deal on A&M Records, but their album failed. Ian went on to became one of the top producer/engineers, going on to work with Jimmy Jam, Terry Lewis, Usher, and Janet Jackson.

The new Woodstock bore no resemblance to the historical event in the '60s. Instead of "Three Days of Peace, Love, and Music," it was more like three days of shirtless guys wearing wrap-around sunglasses drinking Coors Light and creating huge, muddy mosh pits. It was fun, chaotic, and proof positive of an active market of real music fans.

The Goats were a showing a lot of promise. They released their second album, *No Goats, No Glory*. Donnie and the entire staff at Columbia loved this band, and Donnie said at a Columbia Records marketing meeting that the Goats could be the next Rage Against the Machine, a rap-rock group on Columbia's competing sister label, Epic Records. By the time the second album released, Oatie Kato, one of the three original rappers in the Goats, had left the group. I thought Oatie was a weird guy. When the first Goats album came out, my name was conspicuously left out of the special thanks, yet other Ruffhouse people were thanked. It was explained to me that it was Oatie's decision. He told the other group members, "You do not want to be friends with the head of the record company." That one had me scratching my head. Oatie was a great writer, and there were undercurrents questioning whether the repertoire would hold up without Oatie's involvement. I did not agree, but I know that after Oatie left, Joe seemed to lose enthusiasm and regarded the Goats as just another record coming out. The final mixes were not that great, and Joe's response was to just leave them alone.

I told him, "This record is a Ruffhouse release that will get reviewed by *Rolling Stone* and your name is on it. Do you really want to just let it go out there like this?" He acquiesced and went back and fixed the problem areas. The artwork was really cool; it was a graffiti comic book explosion rendering of the album title.

The Goats had been touring in the United States and Europe and had just performed at the Sony Music conference in Miami for the entire Sony Music US group. They wowed everybody, and I felt like we had something really great about to happen. The Goats toured with the Beastie Boys, Public Enemy, Luscious Jackson, and Cypress Hill.

But some members of the Goats had been struggling with drugs and alcohol for some time. We were about to shoot the second video in Philadelphia. We had rented them a van the night before the video shoot so they could get to the different locations, and we gave them per diem money in cash, as well. The next morning, I was getting ready to drive to the shoot when I got a call saying one of the group members took off and disappeared with the van and per diem money to go score crack.

The Goats broke up that day, and that was it.

Two Philadelphia artists, Dandelion and the Goats, both said no to success and imploded. I had huge records out that were selling millions, but these groups were important to me for reasons far beyond financial gains. I was hugely disappointed. I was a true fan of both groups. Not only that, I considered the Goats and Dandelion to be almost like family. They had been to my house on many occasions, and we frequently hung out together.

After Woodstock, Kevon helped me map out new business strategies for Ruffhouse. Kevon and I started attending MIDEM (Marché International du Disque et de l'Edition Musicale) in the south of France. MIDEM is an international music trade show where independent record labels and music publishers from all over the world come together to do deals involving distribution, licensing, and publishing. It is held in Cannes where the Cannes Film Festival is held but at a different time of year. We stayed in beautiful hotels and ate at incredible restaurants, and, obviously, I drank a lot.

When I first attended MIDEM I noticed the lack of hip-hop. But what I loved was being able to come face-to-face with independent label and publishing people from every country. The major labels do not participate at MIDEM because they already have their own international distribution mechanism in place, but just about every independent label and distributor is there. As I was already locked in to Sony, there was not much I could do on the label side, but on the publishing side, I started to pay attention to a revenue source I had been ignoring for too long: music publishing.

There are two major revenue sources in the music business, and music publishing is one of them. Publishing is actually the original source of revenue long before the actual sale of recorded music. In the nineties, record companies made their money from the manufacture, distribution, and sale of vinyl albums and compact discs while publishers made their money from the radio broadcast of songs and the collection of revenues due to songwriters from the physical sale of music (called "mechanical royalties," derived from the days of the player piano). Publishers also, on behalf of the songwriters, collected "synchronization fees" from music used in film and television. When a publisher collects these fees on behalf of the songwriter, it retains a percentage, called an "administration fee," and a portion of the copyright of a song, depending on the agreement between the publisher and the writer. Music publishing companies almost act as banks. They sign a prospective (or established) songwriter to a publishing deal where they give the writer money upfront—an advance against the writer's royalties. The writer, in turn, must deliver a designated number of songs—sides or compositions—which, to qualify as delivered, must be released on a major label or a recognized independent label with major distribution. For example, if the contract period calls for eight covered songs, this means that the writer must get eight of his songs covered by an artist on a major label.

This is easy if the writer also happens to be an artist with a record deal, but for young writers starting out not signed to a label as an artist or in a signed band, the prospect can be daunting, which is why good publishers will "work" their writers. They will set up cowriting sessions with other established writers for the purpose of increasing their chances of getting their songs covered. The contractual commitment for delivery by a writer is usually done in fractions by way of cowrites with other writers. Some hit songs have up to eight different writing contributions, which means multiple publishers collect on it. As a result, it may take a writer sixteen half shares for eight delivered songs, thirty-two quarter shares, etc. It makes no difference. As long as a songwriter's cowriting shares add up to eight covered songs, then he can move on to the next contract period.

Music publishing started with printed sheet music and player piano scrolls in the 1800s. There were music publishing companies long before there were companies in the business of selling packaged, recorded music product. When a production company signs an artist to a recording agreement, it will often take a good part of the publishing, as well. When I signed the production deal with Frank Virtue in the eighties, Frank had typically done what most old school record business people would: he took everything, including ownership of the songs.

By the nineties, the idea of locking an artist into a publishing deal within a recording agreement for a label like Ruffhouse was a nonstarter. Any lawyer with even half a clue would cross it out on the very first draft. There was no reason to give up that revenue source when a record deal on Ruffhouse caused enough for any of the major music publishing companies to offer the prospective artist a six-figure advance.

When we signed an artist to a record deal, I did not think about publishing. I considered myself a record guy, and music publishing was an abstract concept to me. I could not touch it or feel it like a piece of vinyl or a CD. But when we signed the Fugees, somehow we had also made publishing part of the deal, which, looking back, I am surprised David Sonenberg let that one go by. Later, we allowed Sony Music Publishing to buy us out. It was a six-figure check against something I did not really care about at the time.

However, after we moved into the new building, Joe and I decided to start our own publishing company. But things got off to a very rocky start. In order to convince an artist, their management, and the lawyers to allow us to enter into a publishing arrangement, we had to sell them on the idea we could offer all of the services a major music publishing entity could offer, including getting songs placed in film and television, as well as networking the artist with other writers.

Kenny Gamble and Leon Huff had set up Philadelphia International Records with music publishing as a priority from the very start. They were a song-oriented label, and the Broad Street offices had a row of little rooms where the writers would work 24/7, churning out songs until they got a hit. It was like a mining operation looking for gold. We did not have this apparatus as most of our artists were self-contained. They wrote and produced their own material.

So, Joe and I took on a partner, Clare Godholm, who was a music lawyer and Dave Johnson's wife. The idea was to have a credible partner with a background in publishing help us build a foundation as a legitimate publishing company. The venture did not get very far, mainly because Clare was not really suited for the world of hip-hop and R&B, so we disbanded the partnership. The publishing aspect was proving difficult. If we were a little unknown production company, we could get publishing from new artists. But our profile as a label was too big for us to acquire publishing as part of a recording agreement. A record deal with Ruffhouse was cause enough for any major publisher to write a six-figure check.

After we settled in the new building, the third Kris Kross album, *Young, Rich & Dangerous*, went gold, but it definitely did not have the momentum of the first two records and was received with little fanfare. Conversely, the third Cypress Hill record, *Temples of Boom*, did very well as Cypress had solidified a worldwide touring base with a major following. And the Fugees were about to deliver their second record. I do not think anybody was prepared for what was to come. It would forever change the way the world looked at hip-hop.

CHAPTER NINE

READY
OR NOT

The new building was not quite finished, but the business of making records continued. We were still putting the studios together when the Fugees did some mixes for their upcoming release. Although their first record, *Blunted on Reality*, did not make the numbers to put them at recoupment, all indications were this was a group on the rise. But Sony did not quite feel as strongly about the group. The Fugees had performed a show in London where they were plagued with technical problems. Some U.S. Sony executives had attended this show and were overheard saying they did not see a future for this group. Luc Vergier called me the next morning with this news, and I sent a fax to Donnie Ienner saying not only was this group going to happen, they would go on to win Grammys, an absurd claim to make. Around this time, I had been drinking a lot, and when I went out, I had also been doing more than my fair share of cocaine. But I never partied at work.

The Fugees had just spent the better part of the last two years touring off of *Blunted on Reality*. The one thing the Fugees were showing anybody who knew them as artists was how hard they worked. Although Ruffhouse and Sony gave every artist opportunities to evolve, the Fugees also created their own. They camped out on the marketing floor at Sony and were constantly hanging out at Hot 97 in New York, probably the most influential radio station in hip-hop at that time. What people did not understand about the Fugees' juggernaut was this group had made substantial inroads in the United States and Europe before the massive success of the second album.

The biggest problem encountered by artists in promoting records in Europe is that they need to go there and create their own market with little upside at first. Europe is an investment that can pay off in the long term, but you need to go there and do the work. A lot of new hip-hop artists don't like Europe. They often don't like the unfamiliarity of the language, customs, and food. The thought of being outside their comfort zone and working with no immediate financial upside poses a great challenge to them. A new artist often needs to tour in markets with little-to-no audience recognition. European audiences have always been, and will always be, an uncompromising live-music-oriented culture. Their music buying habits are greatly influenced by an artist's live performance rather than radio airplay. Europe has a vast number of festivals where upwards of over a hundred thousand ticket buyers attending is not uncommon. They had been doing this for years. Live performance is one thing Cypress Hill, the Goats, and the Fugees all excelled at in the eyes of the European hip-hop and R&B audience.

I think Joe sometimes questioned why I was always going to Europe, but I know he did not think I was vacationing. As a matter of fact, since the inception of Ruffhouse, I had only ever taken one vacation, and that was when I got married and went on a one-week honeymoon to Puerto Rico. Joe took vacations every year, but I think he always thought my trips to Europe were a needless exercise. He basically spent most or all of his waking hours in the studio when he was not at home. During those years of Ruffhouse, Joe was never one to go to shows or on tours. Up until then, Joe had only seen Cypress Hill and the Fugees perform once, and that was at a special event for Sony where both groups had performed together. But I had been on tours with every Ruffhouse artist.

In the record business, there were four major markets that were crucial to international success: the United Kingdom, France, GSA (the German-speaking territories), and the Netherlands. The United Kingdom was not a huge market in terms of sales, but it was incredibly potent for influencing all of Europe, as well as reversing marketing back to the United States for certain artists. France and Germany were larger markets in terms of volume while the Netherlands was also small in terms of sales, like the United Kingdom. However, due to Rotterdam being a major port, it is an influential gateway to Eastern Europe.

Japan was a huge market but very fickle. Winning over the Japanese audience was challenging for American artists, but if the Japanese like something, they embrace it wholeheartedly, and you can sell an astronomical amount of records there. Early on, the United Kingdom, France, and Germany loved hip-hop and were quick to create their own hip-hop culture with homegrown artists. Germany was always the international heavy metal capital of Europe but took a strong liking to Cypress Hill early on. The Fugees built large audiences in every market, but France was especially receptive to them, due in part to Clef and Pras being Haitian. (Haiti was a French colony, so Wyclef and Pras spoke fluent French, which made French audiences embrace the Fugees as their own.)

The new Fugees album had been in production for some time because, like most groups on the rise, the Fugees never stopped creating new music even when on the road. Muggs, while touring with Cypress Hill, was working with countless other artists, too, as he was having major success with his production company, Soul Assassins. The House of Pain record was doing big numbers.

When the Fugees' new album was finished, the title and artwork were discussed ad nauseum. The Fugees wanted a title that suggested an operatic offering—Clef said something to the effect of calling it *The Libretto*. I am not sure of what conversation it was, but I clearly remember *The Score* being the frontrunner choice, in keeping the original concept. The Fugees wanted the album cover to mimic the lettering and puppet strings used in Mario Puzo's *The Godfather*. We found out this was trademarked by Paramount Pictures, and there would definitely be liability. After the much-publicized Luke Skywalker lawsuit brought upon Luke Skywalker Records in Miami by George Lucas, nobody in the music business even wanted to contemplate a lawsuit with a major film distributor. We ended up doing album artwork with similar lettering but without the puppet strings. We placed in images of the three band members, inspired by the *Goodfellas* movie poster where the main characters' images appeared ominously against a dark background. At the last minute, the Fugees changed their minds about wanting to have their images on the record, but it was too late. Sony had already manufactured and shipped tens of thousands of records.

There was controversy over the choice of the first single, which was to be "Fu-Gee-La." While the single did well, there was no way to keep DJs from playing "Killing Me Softly," the Fugees' remake of Roberta Flack's original. "Killing Me Softly" became an unstoppable behemoth. We shot a video for it, but the group hated it, thinking it looked way too commercial. We ended up shooting a "non-video," which featured the Fugees in a movie theater with other people watching a movie, which were scenes from the original video. It was a completely unintended genius nonsensical mess. The album came out in February of 1996 and was, at that point, the biggest selling Ruffhouse release to date, and there was no stopping it. "Killing Me Softly" became the biggest song in the world and *The Score* sold in droves in every country throughout the world. The Fugees became a bona fide international hip-hop phenomenon.

Ruffhouse's fortunes soared. In March of 1996, I decided to buy a new house, which prompted Myrna and me to start looking at properties in Chester County, Pennsylvania. I was drawn to this area because there were large tracts of land, but ultimately, we decided we did not want to be this far away. We settled on a home in Gladwyne, an affluent area not far from the company office. The home was a beautiful, large white stone house with an attached greenhouse, a guest house, a barn with stables, a riding rink, and a pool. Its main attraction was its location in an area of all deed-restricted land with very few properties near us. The property backed up to a wooded valley with miles of horseback riding trails. I had owned a 1989 Rolls Royce Corniche convertible, which I had restored from the frame up by Harvey Luckman Motor Restorations in New York. It cost 79,000 dollars to restore and was my prize possession. I also owned a number of Bentleys.

I traveled constantly for work between L.A. and New York and took numerous trips to London. Kevon and I went to the south of France for MIDEM every year. I felt I had a good idea of Ruffhouse's value and contribution to Sony's bottom line.

One day, on the plane flying back from the south of France to Paris for a connecting flight to the United States, I sat in a seat in front of Alan Grubman, one of the most powerful people in the music business at that time. He was an attorney whose law firm, Grubman and Indursky, had represented Madonna, Billy Joel, and other major artists. They also represented a number of industry executives, including Sony executives Tommy Mottola and Don Ienner, but also Def Jam and its founder Russell Simmons. They had negotiated Uptown Records founder Andre Harrell's fifty-million-dollar deal with MCA. The firm also had dealings with Ruffhouse, having represented Kris Kross earlier on and renegotiated their recording agreement with us.

I heard over time that the Grubman firm was who you wanted to have when it was time to renegotiate. Kevon was my full-time in-house attorney, but he did not have the political leverage to negotiate a deal that would put Ruffhouse on more balanced footing with Sony.

On the plane, Alan was sitting with his wife. I turned around and introduced myself, told him who I was, and about the millions of dollars his firm had taken from us in Kris Kross's negotiation. He cordially thanked me on behalf of himself and his wife. I expressed interest in having the firm represent Ruffhouse as our contract with Sony needed to be renegotiated. We had renegotiated with Sony twice at that point, but we did not as of yet have the "co-venture" arrangement, which was the Holy Grail for labels like ours.

At that point, we were operating under a production arrangement with Sony. When we originally signed in the beginning, we were given fifteen percent of the net profits, out of which we paid the producer and artist. So, in theory, we would give the artist a deal where they received ten or twelve percent, of which they paid out the producer from their share. This was where it got sticky as the remaining three to five percent or "points" went to Ruffhouse. Sony recouped all of the overhead advances given to Ruffhouse from those three to five points, which was a considerable sum of money, before Ruffhouse saw any profit.

Everything was cross-collateralized, meaning that, along with the overhead, losses from failing projects were deducted from profits of Ruffhouse's share of any successful projects. What often happened was groups like Kris Kross, Cypress Hill, and the Fugees, who sold volume amounts of records, would renegotiate with us, and we, in turn, would renegotiate with Sony for those particular artists, giving the artists additional points, as well as increasing Ruffhouse's profit participation. This was an ongoing situation as we were constantly in some type of negotiation for this artist or that artist. After a number of renegotiations, we had managed to get Ruffhouse's overhead raised to a substantial amount and had increased our spread, as well, but we were far from having a true co-venture with Sony.

A co-venture is when the label and distributor split the revenues 50/50 after deducting expenses. In other words, we would get paid the same as our partner, Columbia Records. Co-venture agreements are not just a contract; the contractual mechanism called for us to actually form a joint venture corporation with Sony. This is something a company like Sony Music Entertainment did not just simply agree to. And, technically, we were already under an agreement with them.

Joe and I went up to New York to meet with Alan Grubman, who introduced us to one of the partners, Paul Schindler, who represented Def Jam, Russell Simmons, and Lyor Cohen. Getting a major to agree to a co-venture was one thing, but the actual technical aspects of it were far beyond what I had imagined.

First, we had to do a full-on business plan with a proposed release schedule with profit projections, both domestically and internationally. This required the services of a CPA firm that specialized in music business accounting. Paul introduced us to Burt Padell, an industry veteran accountant. He represented major music artists, actors, and athletes. His offices in New York had one of the biggest collections of sports memorabilia I had ever seen. From the lobby to the hallways was this incredible amount of sports memorabilia that must have been worth millions of dollars. We met in his conference room, which had wall-to-wall hanging baseball bats—hundreds of them. It was nuts. Burt set about explaining that, when auditing a major label, the key place to consider is the international revenue reports. Underreported royalties are not intentional. But when there is a renegotiation, simple things like royalty bumps may not be added in the computerized accounting mechanisms and this can cause miscalculations upwards of tens of thousands to hundreds of thousands of dollars, especially when your company does the international volume we were doing. Burt's company set about putting together the data we needed to create the business plan. We finally did secure a co-venture, but only for new artists going forward and any solo projects from existing group artists.

Afterwards, I went out to L.A. for the video shoot for the second Fugees single, "Ready or Not," directed by Marcus Nispel. It was a whole extravaganza involving helicopters, artillery, jet skis, motorcycles, jeeps, artillery and a submarine. The premise of the video was Clef was being held captive by an army group on an island and needed to be rescued by Ms. Hill and Pras in a submarine. This was quite an undertaking. The submarine scenes were shot at Fox Studios, Warner, and Paramount Pictures. At Fox, an actual WWII submarine in movable sections was used to shoot interiors.

The outside ocean scenes were shot at the Paramount process lake, which was a big pond with a backdrop that looked like the horizon. The top half shell of the submarine was towed around the lake. The crew then agitated the water with motorboats and sprayed artificial rain from water cannons, creating the illusion of being in the ocean in stormy conditions. The scuba scenes were shot with stunt doubles at Warner Brothers in a large circular aquarium. The magic of cinematography and editing created this fantastic video, which raised the video production bar for everybody else. The final tally of costs was somewhere close to three million dollars, but this project was more than deserving of this level of production. The Fugees were redefining hip-hop. "Ready or Not" was a major hit record throughout all Europe, right on the heels of "Killing Me Softly." The song was a partial remake of the Delfonics' "Ready or Not Here I Come" and a track from Enya entitled "Boadicea." The Enya portion was not cleared ahead of time. This was bad as the album had already sold over two million copies in the United States alone and was selling by the tons in Europe. Enya, however, was very gracious in not bringing a suit but settled for a large six-figure advance against the newly issued interpolation.

Although Ruffhouse had some dysfunctions internally, it was now definitely defined as one of the top hip-hop labels in the world. Jeff Wells was a lighting guy who had come to the building to do some electrical work when we were rehabbing our new space. I'd seen Jeff around for years at gigs in Philly; he always had a silver road case carrying his lighting tools. We became friendly. Jeff's level of maturity and organizational abilities made him a shoe-in to work for us, and he soon became the general manager for the label. Like any other label, this job was really the designated shit catcher; his job was to take some of the day-to-day minutia off of my desk and help keep everybody happy. He was very helpful in the early days of the Fugees' second album release, keeping things organized within the label.

But Ruffhouse was no different from other companies, and I constantly dealt with interoffice politics. Kevon Glickman and Rich Murray both had spent a great deal of time previously working in their respective fields in New York—Rich in film production and Kevon in entertainment law. I brought Rich back to Philadelphia to head up Ruffhouse's film production, which eventually evolved into a feature film company. Jeff Coulter was in charge of administration; this was not an easy job. He was responsible for all of the budgeting, book keeping, payroll, and A&R administration, which meant he was in charge of all of the production budgets and making sure that, when we delivered an album to Sony, all of the correct timings, song credits, and contractual advances were paid to the artists, producers, and managers.

We would not get the budgets from Sony unless all this information was delivered along with the masters. Record releases are set up with a release date, and then it goes backwards to determine when project elements need to be delivered to make sure the release date is kept. All this was tied in with the marketing plans, which were jointly put together between Ruffhouse and Sony. This involved everybody on the Ruffhouse side, including Jeff Wells who was General Manager, and Rob Dippold (who worked right under Jeff Wells but would later replace him). Glenn Manko did publicity, Rose Mann did retail marketing, Rich Murray oversaw video production, and Evan Gusz handled our rock artists (Dandelion, Trip 66, and other artists we were developing). Tamara Feldman and Stephanie Locke did everything that was needed. All of this was supported by an army of interns, and everything was overseen by me.

This was a 24/7 gig. These people were my family. Everybody was totally loyal to the cause, but, like all families, there was always inner strife. Much of it revolved around Kevon Glickman and Rich Murray. They were much alike in that they both took their chosen professions seriously, but their personalities did not mesh well with other people. Kevon had a very business-like approach and would unintentionally rub people the wrong way. Rich, on the other hand, was very impatient with people and often times would treat people as yokels who did not deserve their jobs. Kevon and Rich would often not get along, and this was a constant source of irritation for me. Funny enough, although Joe and I definitely had different points of view on a lot of things, never once since the inception of the label did we exchange words in a harsh manner. But these guys could not even pretend to indulge in any cordiality for the shortest amount of time. However, I tried my best to make things work for everybody, as they were my friends, and we depended on each other.

Kevon was representing an EDM (electronic dance music) artist named Josh Wink. Josh was a techno DJ and very popular in Europe with a big-selling single, "Size 9." DJs were just starting to come into their own as bona fide recording artists.

The mid-'90s were the early days of EDM, which would later be made popular by artists like the Chemical Brothers, The Prodigy, and Moby. Josh had a partner named King Britt, who was formerly the DJ for the hip-hop group Digable Planets. Josh and King formed a production company called Ovum Records, and Kevon was campaigning for me to enter into a deal with Josh to sign him and Britt as artists and to bring Ovum Records under the Ruffhouse/Sony distribution banner. At first, I was skeptical, but Kevon made an interesting case: Josh did sell a lot of singles and was also getting serious money being booked to do raves both in the United States and internationally. However, for me, the most influential factor in making the deal was that I did not consider EDM to be that far away from the music Jeff Coulter and I had performed together in the early eighties. I was excited to be involved in the early stages of what I considered a new, credible genre. I also had the support of Muff Winwood, a high-level Sony exec in London. Muff is Steve Winwood's brother, and he was in charge of a new division of Sony in Europe, which was to specialize in newer genres of music. Donnie was on board, so we set about doing this deal.

This was not an inexpensive endeavor; the idea was that we would have Josh and Britt as artists and as a label. Britt made a great record under this deal called *Sylk 130*, which was never a big seller for us but, to this day, has been reissued by many smaller labels in the dance market. The deal called for us to fund Ovum as a label with not only recording budgets for Josh and King but also a commitment to release artists they deliver. This seemed like a smart, one-stop shopping move to get a foothold in this genre.

My biggest problem from the start was Josh was a little difficult. I had been doing this for a number of years, and I had
dealt with all sorts of artists and their personalities, but Josh
wanted me to jump through hoops. Even though there were
other labels offering him a deal, they were not offering what
we were. Before Josh would sign with us, he wanted to have a
personal one-on-one meeting with Donnie, which kind of had
me scratching my head since he'd never deal directly with
Donnie. But I did not give a shit; it was about Josh getting his
ego stroked. Donnie agreed, and we went to New York where
Donnie met with Josh and King in a conference room for
about a half hour.

After the meeting, Donnie came out, pulled me aside in the
hallway, and said, "They are DJs."

I understood what he was expressing. DJs were not yet the
new rock stars they would become years later. Spending all of
this money on a couple of DJs who had no label infrastructure,
no immediate records to market and distribute, and no real
album sales track record was definitely a gamble. On top of
this, we were funding them as an A&R source. After we signed
the contracts, which were for a boatload of money, we were all
set anticipating Josh's album. We took Josh to MIDEM and
then to a dance music conference where he spoke at a panel.
All of this hoopla involved Sony in New York and the United
Kingdom for this big, anticipated release.

Shortly after those trips, Josh and King came into the office
one day with their label manager, Matt, and played us a demo
tape of this mediocre R&B singer. This was who they wanted
as their first signing. I did not understand it at all. First off, the
proposed artist was nowhere near the caliber of what was
needed to compete in the market. Second, we did not need
Ovum to bring us R&B; we could do that on our own. The

Fugees had the biggest R&B, pop, hip-hop record in the world. Ruffhouse had that covered. What we needed was the Josh Wink album so we could set up Ovum for its intended purpose as a premier label within this genre.

King Britt's *Sylk 130* album, although it did not do well sales-wise, was a great record with a very cool packaging concept. Years later, I met people in Europe who told me they had licensed it from this label as part of some deal with somebody else. This happened more than once as King's record stayed alive for a long time in the underground dance scene.

Ovum signed an artist named Jamie Myerson, who did an EDM album that did respectable numbers, given its budget. But we really needed a Josh Wink record, and Muff Winwood was waiting for it as well.

At one point, Josh said, "I am just waiting for the Chemical Brothers and Moby to 'blow over.'" So when he did deliver his much-anticipated album, there would be no other distractions in the marketplace? After about a year and probably a million dollars later, Josh finally gave us the album, which came out with very little fanfare. Muff Winwood said Josh waited too long; there was so much anticipation and excitement, but that was a year ago—a lifetime in the world of dance music. This was a very expensive lesson for me.

Truth be told, I went into this deal not listening to my gut but really getting caught up in Kevon's hype. I felt like I got burned, but I didn't blame Kevon, I blamed myself. On top of that, later on I found it interesting that anytime Ovum was interviewed in the press, they talked as though Ovum was directly distributed by Sony with no mention whatsoever of Ruffhouse, even though I was the one who paid for their entire deal, which was recouped against our revenues by Sony.

I made a substantial investment in something I did not completely understand; I let my excitement for an emerging genre cloud my judgment. There were warning bells from the very beginning that this was not a label, and even Josh's lawyer said, "Let's face it, you are giving Josh a label deal in order to sign him as an artist." The audience, transient and fickle, had moved on. Moby went on to be a big pop star, and other artists, like Daft Punk, redefined the entire genre. I made a bad deal; lesson learned.

CHAPTER TEN

GONE TIL NOVEMBER

n 1996, Jeff Wells and I went to the MTV Music Video Awards where the Fugees' "Killing Me Softly" was nominated for best video. Like a lot of affairs, they packed a bunch of celebrities in an auditorium and broadcast it on TV. I had been to tons of MTV Awards shows and Grammy Award ceremonies, but I was excited to see the Fugees perform. The Fugees performed the song with Roberta Flack. I sat with Whitney Houston during rehearsals. There was an after party, and Jeff and I hung out there with Chris Farley. It was a very late night.

The next morning, I woke up in the hotel hungover and asked Jeff Wells for some aspirin. Jeff always kept with him a metal briefcase and a knapsack carrying anything and everything. He fumbled around in his knapsack and handed me two pills. He told me they were Tylenol 4s, and they had codeine in them. He had had major dental surgery a few weeks previous and had a lot of them. I popped them in my mouth and laid down. Within a half hour, not only did I feel better, I felt like I could do anything. I had this warm, numb feeling, which was caused by the active component codeine flooding my opiate receptors. Because I had overdosed on heroin years before, I was always very careful to stay away from anything opiate related. But I was soon hitting up Jeff for more until I went through his entire prescription.

A few weeks later, a producer friend of mine gave me a Percocet, and I was addicted. Like a lot of addicts, I thought I could keep it under control. Soon I was buying and using it frequently, until the point where I would go through withdrawal if I did not have it. I was an avid consumer of Percocet and Vicodin. This became a new problem for me, and it was only exacerbated by the ease of which I could acquire the drug. I would never actually go buy them; I would have them brought to me, or I would pay somebody to go get them. I took them in the morning when I got up just to feel normal. Since I did not buy them directly from a dealer, I paid a steep surcharge, but I did not care. Worse yet, I often took them with alcohol. I had to have them. Myrna caught on to this one a lot quicker than I thought.

There were periods when the pills were not available, and when product availability is low, prices go up. Nothing was worse than going up to New York for meetings while going through withdrawal, but my habit was getting expensive. When I went to L.A., I had them sent to my hotel via FedEx. So simple math and practicality led me down a well-traveled road taken by many addicted to opium: I eventually opted for the less expensive, more readily available heroin. Funny that ten years ago, people were spreading lies about me taking heroin. Now, it became my truth.

This was a new enemy in my long-term battle with self-medicating. Dope was an effective way to mask the inner trauma I had suffered since childhood. But, as they say in recovery, to win, you need to avoid people, places, and things. This was going to be difficult. Heroin was making a big comeback, replacing cocaine as the new drug of choice. I would convince myself I was not going to let it slow me down, but I was only fooling myself. One of the biggest challenges when somebody becomes addicted is that they tend to associate with other addicts, which makes it difficult to get clean. There were no other dope addicts working at Ruffhouse, but I had no shortage of facilitators.

I was living, eating, and breathing the record business. All I cared about was making records. I had money, but I did not take vacations or do any of the things other people in the business did to spend it. I did not go on ski vacations to Aspen or go scuba diving in Hawaii. Although I had an extensive designer wardrobe, along with over 150 pairs of shoes, most of the time I dressed in jeans and T-shirts, unless I was going into meetings. My only real material vice was my cars.

Joe and I decided to give it another go in creating a new publishing company. I had relatively recently befriended a woman named Deirdre O'Hara, who ran Sony Music's West Coast office. Deirdre was an industry veteran and a huge fan of R&B. I saw her at MIDEM and visited with her when I went to L.A. Deirdre had a house in Hollywood where she would host parties with all sorts of writers, and she had a place in New York City, too. Myrna and I once hung out in Ireland with her and her friends who were all part of U2's management. In L.A., we went to a U2 concert together with Nicolas Cage.

When Deirdre's contract came to an end with Sony Music, we brought her on to head up our publishing company under EMI. We opened up an office in downtown New York. But, despite Deirdre's talent and capabilities, the company was almost immediately top-heavy with overhead. When Deirdre was with Sony Music as a top executive, she had received a significant salary in keeping with her responsibilities and had vast resources. The challenge for Deirdre was trying to get her accustomed to doing more with less. After her salary and the rent on the office, equipment, and staff, there was little-to-no funding left.

Round two at a publishing company was unfortunately a very short-lived venture, and I blamed myself for not thinking it through enough beforehand. We never did get it together to have a full-fledged publishing company, but I tried to sign some artists to publishing deals when we entered into recording agreements going forward. It was not to get any easier.

THE FUGEES' ALBUM, *The Score*, had resonated worldwide, selling unprecedented numbers. It went platinum in every country throughout the world, and in some countries multiplatinum. It was a global phenomenon offering something for everybody, particularly in the Caribbean, in part because the island influenced musical components of the Fugees' repertoire. The Fugees were worldwide superstars, and it was not surprising that Wyclef and Pras's homecoming to Haiti was like the Beatles coming back home to England after conquering America.

Before the news coverage of the earthquake in 2010, most people never gave Haiti much thought, other than that it was one of the poorest countries in the world, sharing an island with the more tourist-attractive Dominican Republic. I have been to some of the poorest parts of the United States and Europe, including the worst ghettos on both continents, and parts of Appalachia, where people live in total austerity fueled by the machinations of the coal mining industry and government. But even that could never have prepared me for the poverty of Haiti, where, on my first visit, I could not stop wondering how a country like this could exist in a modern world. Like most Caribbean islands, Haiti thrived on tourism, as well as the agricultural industry, but its tourism sector fell behind while other Caribbean countries flourished.

At one time, Haiti was considered to be an exclusive getaway for the very wealthy. There still are remnants of once-spectacular hotels, enclaves of splendor with European architecture. They were beautiful retreats surrounded by manicured gardens with cobblestone approach roads. These magnificent structures have long fallen into decay and ruin. Due to corruption in the system of government post-World War II, Haiti fell to political discord and civil unrest, causing the international tourism trade to leave the country virtually discarded.

I had been to Haiti before, when we shot the "Fu-Gee-La" video, but this trip was different. When we disembarked off the plane at the Port-au-Prince airport, tens of thousands of Haitians were there to welcome the Fugees. The little airport at the time was no more imposing than a local municipal airport you would find in the midwestern United States. There was one airliner that came and left twice a day and a corrugated steel building that served as a terminal.

Due to a very inadequate public works infrastructure, there were not many roads in the country accessible without the use of an all-wheel drive vehicle. One night, we were climbing up a road on the side of a mountain in a torrential storm in a caravan of SUVs. I watched out the window as the road washed away down the side of the hill as we were driving. There was no phone service; most people who could afford it used limited cell service. The most common method of long-distance personal communication was the physical delivery of messages and house-to-house coverage by two-way radio.

When we arrived, national police bodyguard units were assigned to each of us for personal security. Some of these guys were so diligent they would follow me into the bathroom. I could understand this was a big event for them as the Fugees were there to do a show to benefit the people of Haiti. Getting around was a major operation. We were driven around in big SUVs with the police escorts. There were hundreds of radio stations on our stop in Port-au-Prince. I didn't get it at first. How could there be so many stations? The answer was that each station covered only a very small area. The broadcast wattage would only extend for an area the size of a few city blocks. Clef did not neglect a single one of them.

Despite the infrastructure woes and the general poverty, Haiti also had some very uniquely charming aspects. Although the hotels we stayed at had razor wire security fencing and an employee guarding the entrance with an assault weapon, I woke up every morning to roosters crowing. The roosters would sometimes perch themselves right on my window ledge. Goats, pigs, and chickens all wandered around untethered. It was explained to me that everybody knew what belonged to who, and it was extremely rare for people to steal each other's animals.

Haiti, like most Third World countries, had a stray dog population. There were thousands of them everywhere. It was really depressing, especially realizing that, in a country where people are struggling, the welfare of animals was low on the list of national concern. Dogs were routinely poisoned by people who saw them simply as nuisances.

The Haitian people were by far and large friendly and joyful, especially considering the circumstances that the majority of them lived in. Most lived in shanties—little corrugated steel shelters—tens of thousands deep as far as the eye could see. I saw mothers washing clothes in puddles beside the road and fathers leading a single goat or cow about.

Most of the schools were Catholic schools, and the kids wore uniforms similar to what I wore as a young child at St. Monica's. One day, on our way somewhere, a large group of young kids in their uniforms walked past Clef and me. Clef turned to me.

"That was me when I was a young child growing up here," he said.

Haiti gave me a better picture of Wyclef and Pras as artists. To be an entertainer in Haiti, you needed to be more than just a singer or instrumentalist. Most entertainers in Haiti, like most Third World countries, made their living in the streets, and you needed to be multifaceted. You needed to dance, juggle, and do acrobatics to earn money. Clef carried this early training with him when he came to the States. Clef stood apart from others in the hip-hop world because, besides being a musician, singer, and writer, he was an all-around entertainer.

The Haitian benefit show was held in an arena that was created using big cargo containers the size of railroad cars. The containers were stacked three high encircled around a huge area the size of several football fields, creating this huge, makeshift coliseum. We were issued bulletproof vests by the UN unit that was assigned to look after us. The concert was attended by well over 100,000 Haitians—the most enthusiastic crowd I had ever seen. By that time, the Fugees had over three years of touring experience and had created an incredible live show like nothing else in hip-hop. After the show, which was to benefit Haiti, the only people who benefited were the government officials who took possession of the proceeds. But overall, the event solidified Wyclef as, arguably, the most famous Haitian in the world at that time.

While in Haiti, we went to the palace to meet the president, and Clef introduced me to a number of popular Haitian artists. One of them was Michel "Sweet Micky" Martelly who, later, after the earthquake, won a presidential election in which Clef also was a candidate but was disqualified for his passport not showing five years of continuous Haitian residency. Micky was a Carnival musician. Carnival is a music festival held every year throughout the Caribbean where the musicians perform traditional music on parade floats. It was during this trip that Clef and I talked about doing an independent record of traditional Haitian music infused with elements of pop.

When we returned home, Clef started working on this record that I was personally funding. We were not going to put it out on Ruffhouse as a frontline release, but through an independent distribution network. I was intending to present it to Chris Blackwell, the founder of Island Records. Island Records was the home to such artists as Bob Marley, who, after signing with Chris Blackwell, became the most iconic music star in the world, even to this day. Some people will argue Elvis, Michael Jackson, and the Beatles hold that title, but Bob Marley's image is recognized in more places on earth than any other music artist.

Chris Blackwell is a Jamaican native and started Island Records as an independent label in 1959. His first record was the single "My Boy Lollipop" by Millie Small, a young Jamaican girl. The record went to the top of the charts in the United States and Great Britain, and Island Records became synonymous with reggae music throughout the world. It was not until Chris signed Steve Winwood, who Chris credited with giving Island prestige among rock artists, that Island became one of the top record companies in the world. Chris's creative and business acumen made Island Records a respected marquee name in the music industry.

In 1993, I was introduced to Chris in New York; we became friends, and he was somebody I always called for advice. Myrna and I even took trips to Jamaica to stay at his house in Golden Eye, a resort he owned that was formerly the home of Ian Fleming, author of the James Bond books. He was a great friend and a valuable resource whenever I was in a negotiation. Chris was great at explaining major label economics and how the majors really made their money. He was the first one to point out to me that, although manufacturing was a cost borne by the label, the majors, since they owned the manufacturing, profited on that component, as well as on the distribution. He pointed out that these costs, which Ruffhouse was charged back for, contributed to their corporate bottom line. Later, Chris told me that he was very upset that Island had passed on the Fugees. He rightfully said, "The Fugees would have been perfect for Island."

As Clef's record progressed, it was no longer an independent record of traditional music but started to become something else. Musically, it resembled a Fugees record, but it was totally conceived by Clef. It was soon obvious this would be a Wyclef solo record involving a bigger budget, so we exercised the option in the Fugees' agreement for this being a solo project. Per this contract clause, all Ruffhouse recording agreements involving more than one artist, like a rock band or rap group, were signed by each artist in the group "singularly and collectively," meaning, should one member of a group decide to move on to a solo record, the artist was contractually bound to Ruffhouse. I was very excited about the new Wyclef record, but the project was not without its hurdles.

In 1997, with the new Ruffhouse offices and the studios completed, we looked at securing some new artists. One of those was Kool Keith, a member of a popular hip-hop group called Ultramagnetic MCs. Keith had made a record with producer Dan "Automator" Nakamura called *Dr. Octagon*. The record was probably, in my humble estimation, one of the most innovative hip-hop records I had ever heard. The beats were reminiscent of the early Schoolly D records and Cypress Hill. On the record, Kool Keith was featured as an alter ego, aptly called Dr. Octagon, and he gave an absurdist narrative throughout the entire record. It was captivatingly funny, with references to science fiction and porn. I thought this was a perfect record for Ruffhouse for many reasons.

But oddly I could not get Sony on board. The black music marketing department did not get it, but why did they have to? This was an age-old problem, the same I had with Schoolly D and Cypress Hill in the beginning, who both had a predominately white audience. Simply put, marketing did not know how to approach these audiences. *Dr. Octagon* was a quintessential alternative hip-hop record, but because they could not understand it, I could not get the funding to do the project. It ended up coming out on an indie label and was immediately embraced by college radio. *Rolling Stone* magazine had it as a top ten college radio album. Later on, the record got picked up by DreamWorks.

We did end up signing Kool Keith as he was probably in our estimation unique in that he was a veteran of the early days of hip-hop and had created a cult following. Ultramagnetic MCs were influential in defining hip-hop in the eighties. Keith doing *Dr. Octagon* all these years later proved that he was innovative and could reinvent himself. Even though we couldn't do the *Dr. Octagon* record, we were not dissuaded in working with Keith so we signed him and released the album *Black Elvis/Lost in Space*. It was produced by Keith and featured tracks by Roger Troutman, Kid Capri, and KutMasta Kurt. It was different from *Dr. Octagon* but contained some very cool musical elements. The release date was pushed back numerous times because of label copy and other administrative issues. We eventually released it through the independent RED distribution because we felt we could get better traction at retail.

We also signed a group out of Yonkers called Sporty Thievz, who had done an answer record called "No Pigeons," a track giving the male point of view in response to TLC's "No Scrubs." The group was signed to a label called Roc-A-Block, owned by Darien Dash, a cousin to Damon Dash. Damon was Jay Z's partner in Roc-A-Fella. "No Pigeons" went gold with 500,000 copies sold, and we did an album called *Street Cinema* with a video for the single "Cheapskate," featuring another new Ruffhouse artist, Liz Leite. Rich Murray directed it. We shot part of it in a studio in Delaware, which had an innovative camera system. The camera was on a robotic arm that was centered in a circular studio. The video showed the performers in a continuous shot as though there was no editing. Liz Leite was a rapper from Brooklyn who had been getting a lot of attention. I had a meeting with Donnie and Tone and Poc, the new heads of the Columbia Records black music department, to discuss Liz. A dispute over Liz's signing dollar amount occurred at the meeting. It was a feeble attempt to try to make it look like I overpaid for an artist they could have signed for less. This was nothing new, just label politics and people trying to protect their jobs.

One time, I was in an elevator with two college-age guys who were complaining about working at Epic Records. As I got off, I asked them what they did. One replied he did A&R, and the other said he worked in video production. I told them they had no idea how lucky they were, and I walked away. As the owner of Ruffhouse Records, the most successful distributed label in the history of CBS and Sony Music, their comments shouldn't have irked me. But it bothered me that somebody at that age could complain about something I considered a privilege.

The Wyclef solo record was almost done, but we had a few challenges. Clef called me on a Tuesday with David Sonenberg on the phone. He wanted to record a song called "Gone till November" with an orchestra. The budget from Sony had not yet been released, but Clef had already booked the eighty-piece orchestra for that Thursday. I agreed to front out the monies. Then I met with Donnie that day to play him a few of the tracks from the record. He listened to a few songs and handed back the CD. He was not impressed, and I felt it was not the right time to tell him about the eighty-piece orchestra. Sony thought everyone would be better served with a new Fugees record. While I did not disagree, Wyclef was going to make this record with or without us.

When the Wyclef record was finished, we discussed the album title. We talked about the original idea behind it—about the Caribbean influence, Carnival, and everything else that started the project in the first place. And there the title was right in front of us: *The Carnival.* The record came out, and it was embraced by worldwide audiences. Even years later, the album appears on numerous top ten album picks.

The video for "Gone till November" was brilliant as it featured a cameo appearance by Bob Dylan, who as it turned out was a Wyclef fan. Since Bob Dylan was a Columbia Records artist, Donnie Ienner reached out to him ask if he would be in the video, and Bob agreed to do it. *The Carnival* made Wyclef one of the most sought-after artists for features, and he was suddenly one of the hottest producers in music. Other tracks, "Guantanamera" and "We Trying to Stay Alive," also had amazing videos with cameo performances by Ms. Hill and Pras. The album sold over five million copies worldwide in the first year and won two Grammy Awards. I was immensely proud of this record. The Fugees were now recognized as the hottest franchise in music.

But now there was tremendous pressure all around for another Fugees album. Quite simply, a new Fugees record would probably ship three to four million records worldwide in the first week alone. That type of anticipated revenue caused a lot of conversation and speculation.

Wyclef turned his attention to producing an album by John Forté, a member of the Refugee Camp featured on *The Score* and *The Carnival.* The album was called *Poly Sci* and featured Fat Joe and DMX. Forté did an interview in the *New York Times* where he talked about his education at Phillips Exeter Academy. This interview sparked controversy among the hip-hop audience because it bucked the widespread belief that rap artists were not supposed to be educated (despite many successful hip-hop artists who were also college graduates).

Unfortunately, in the process of creating the album, there was an undercurrent of drama between John Forté and Wyclef. I could never get a straight answer as to what it involved. And, despite Clef's production and John's association with the Fugees, the album which came out in early 1998 sold just north of 100,000 copies. John was later on arrested with a large quantity of cocaine and was charged and sentenced for intent to distribute. Thanks to Carly Simon, who petitioned senators and congressmen, John received a presidential pardon and was later released.

We signed some other artists through Muggs's Soul Assassins label. Call O' Da Wild and Psycho Realm were offshoots of the Cypress Hill phenomenon, and we got lots of traction at both retail and radio. Psycho Realm lyrically talked about subjects explored on the Cypress Hill records. However, the group, although talented, did not have the magical elements to drive record sales like that of Cypress Hill. Also, because of the association with Cypress, the barometer was set very high. Call O' Da Wild was featured on the Cypress Hill *Unreleased and Revamped* album track called "Intellectual Dons." Again, the group had the lyrical goods and the production was there, but they did not quite measure up to the expectations of their association with Cypress Hill.

Fugees member Pras made a solo record called *Ghetto Superstar*, which, although it did not perform commercially on the level of Clef's album, was nominally thought to be a good record overall. The title track, "Ghetto Superstar," featuring Mya and Ol' Dirty Bastard, was a bona fide worldwide hit but could not generate the retail movement for the album. I think the biggest issue was that, although Pras definitely was the one who brought the Fugees together and had come up with ideas for their biggest tracks, he alone could not carry a record to meet the expectations of what people expected, sales-wise, from a Fugee. We spent over a million dollars on a video shot by filmmaker Antoine Fuqua (who went on to make the film *Training Day*). The video was shot on a battleship and featured Pras as a secret agent operative. The exorbitant costs associated with both the video and the advances for the album mitigated any true monetary success the album saw. I should have tried to get this project reeled in, but it was very difficult to manage egos and expectations, especially when a project involved an artist as big as Pras. It's very difficult to tell them what they can and cannot do.

The professional rollercoaster that took over my life during this period spilled over into my personal life. I was trying to keep my drug habit in check, but, in 1998, I finally went into a program at the Caron Foundation in Pennsylvania. I checked in over Christmas, as I thought this would be a good time to disappear since the entertainment industry basically shuts down for two weeks over the Christmas holiday. But my time in Caron was not easy.

After spending time in the detox unit, I found myself in the cafeteria at a table with a bunch of kids in their early twenties. They were talking about their favorite hip-hop groups, and Cypress Hill came up. They talked about which Cypress Hill shows they had been to. One of them even had a Cypress Hill logo tattooed on his arm, which he proudly displayed to everybody. I did not say anything; I really just wanted to go home. Rehab is hard when you are used to staying in the nicer hotels. I was not into sharing a room with a stranger. But these places are there to give you what you need, not what you want. The hardest thing for me wasn't not having access to drugs and alcohol, but dealing with the boredom. I could not read anything other than materials dealing with recovery. Since I was a child, I had always been a voracious reader, and I would always have books, especially on the road. When I checked into Caron, they took my books.

The program was to span thirty days, but I left eight days early. I wanted to get back to work. I had hired a trainer and put an exercise bike in the office. It was the first time in over ten years I had been alcohol and drug free. Which was why it

surprised me that I was starting to feel a certain distance oc-
curring between Joe and me. We had started out as just the
two of us, but now we both had multitudes of people under us.
What a lot of people had said over the years was it was completely surprising that Joe and I never had even one argument.
Even though we both had done things which pissed each other
off, we were experts at both looking the other way. We had it
down to a science. I think looking back that this company
started as something neither Joe or I could ever have dreamed
would be so successful. I don't think that success was causing
animosity, but we just did not communicate on a personal level
as we did in the early years.

I always thought Joe was easily one of the most talented producers in the hip-hop world, in the same league as Arthur
Baker and Rick Rubin. He saw early on what other producers
would later emulate. For example, in the early days of hip-hop
production, most studio guys tried to make the drum sounds
clean and antiseptic, but Joe went the other way; he understood the appeal of giving drum tracks a crunchy, bombastic
feel, almost what seasoned producers considered as being a
counterintuitive approach to production. Later, as Ruffhouse
became a major player in the hip-hop game, Joe had carved
out a nice little gig for himself. He spent the day recording
music for other record companies in his own production studio, getting paid handsomely and collecting his share of monies as half-owner of Ruffhouse.

Joe's exceptional talents and capabilities in the control
room maybe distracted him from ever really understanding
the workings of the label and the process we had put together
with Sony to market and promote our artists on a global platform. We had been with Sony for ten years as our distributor.
Yet Joe had limited knowledge of the inner workings of Sony

Music. I never left him out, but I think he never wanted to be bothered. I'd call him at home to talk to him about a Ruffhouse issue, only to talk for a minute before he cut me off and said he had to go. It was about the mid-nineties when I finally stopped calling Joe at home unless it was a DEFCON-level issue. His concerns were centered around making a quality product to maximize profit while minimizing time and effort.

But occasionally, Joe would make comments about employees at the label that did bother me.

"Chris will hire anybody off a barstool," he'd say. I never hired anybody I met in a bar or nightclub. Yes, I partied a lot, and yes, I had problems, but I built this machine by working 24/7 for Ruffhouse. He would occasionally talk about "Righting the ship back on course." Well the ship was on course, and the most anticipated record in the world was about to come out.

Tsunami. Dead ahead...

CHAPTER ELEVEN

1998: BATH, ENGLAND

Phones in England have double rings. The phone in the hotel room where I was staying was loud and jarring, especially at three in the morning. I had to look for it as the room was pitch black, and I did not want to turn the light on with Myrna sleeping next to me. Before going to sleep, I had a habit of covering every light source with towels and clothes. I covered every light source on phones, digital clocks, smoke alarms, TVs, and laptops. Windows were especially a challenge. I pulled down the blinds and closed the drapes, but that was never enough. I used extra sheets and comforters to block out streetlights or any early morning day-light. If the room was not pitch black, then the tiniest light source would wake me, a lasting after-effect of a long-term addiction to opiates: not being able to sleep.

The phone kept ringing while I fumbled around in the dark. I knew who was calling. My cell was turned off, and the only people who had my itinerary were Joanie, who managed my household, and Donnie's office. Joanie would not have called at three in the morning United Kingdom time, but the powers at Sony Music were not that concerned about time zones, especially given the reason for the call.

Before I left on this trip, I had given them the long-awaited first five rough mixes of songs from Ms. Lauryn Hill's forthcoming solo record, and I'm sure they had some commentary. I was a little apprehensive to be talking straight out of a dead sleep; I would have preferred to have this conversation when I was coherent and rested. The fact they were calling me at three in the morning was not a good sign. I spent over two million dollars of Sony's money on this production so far, not including Ms. Hill's advance on profits, and I was sure they had a lot to say.

Her project was easily the most anticipated record in the world, and I had been walking a tightrope, spinning plates for over a year trying to run interference while she finished this project. Everything was working against this record in terms of major label politics. First, Sony had come to terms with the fact she would not participate in a new Fugees project anytime in the foreseeable future. Secondly, Sony didn't trust nor believe she could write and produce this record on her own. They wanted this album to be written and produced by proven marquee name producers to ensure their investment. They pitched Puffy, the RZA, and other major producers. But, ultimately, this was her project to do.

Traditionally, albums made by multiple writers and producers have always been the time-honored methodology in R&B. But, in this case, multiple outside producers would have been cookie cutter and predictable. Sure, her star power alone would make it a platinum record guaranteed, but there would have been nothing special about it. Besides that, Ruffhouse was an artist-oriented label. We never had any real success with producer-driven projects, which was why we always looked for self-contained artists. This was a gamble, but if she pulled this off, the rewards would be astronomical. I was willing to roll the dice, but this phone call was to remind me I was playing with the house's money.

I picked up the phone and sat at the edge of the bed. Donnie's receptionist, Kim, asked me to hold for Donnie. Donnie came on the line sounding like he was in a cave. He was on speakerphone with other people in the room listening to our conversation. This sucked, as I had no idea who was there.

"Tommy and I listened to the Lauryn tracks," he started. Shit, now I knew who was in the room: Tommy Mottola, head of Sony Music worldwide and Donnie's boss.

"Tommy and I think the songs are very, very, very mediocre."

They did not like the record thus far. Great—not that I expected different. They did not like a lot of things at first, and I think they anticipated not liking it because their producers weren't attached to it. It was an amalgamation of hip-hop, seventies soul, and pop with mostly live instrumentation. I gave Donnie a few short answers and reminded him the record was not done yet. I loved Donnie, but I could not wait to get off this call. He asked me when I was getting back to the States and hung up. I sat there at the foot of the bed, thinking.

I did not want to tell Myrna about Sony because we were having such a great time, but I could not go back to sleep after that call. Myrna and I were on a short getaway in England taking in the sights. I had business in London, and afterwards we visited friends. We rented a car to travel the English countryside. We went to Bath to see the underground springs and the Roman bathhouse ruins.

Unable to sleep, I grabbed a book and went down to the lobby to read for a while. I sat in the lobby and tried to read, but I kept reading the same paragraph four or five times before I gave up. I could not concentrate. The phone call from Sony kept replaying in my head like an endless loop: "Very, very, very mediocre."

I knew the record was awesome, but sometimes beauty is in the eye of the beholder, and I was not only the CEO of the record label, I was a fan, and sometimes in that position, I knew I could get tunnel vision. If the phone call was from anybody but two of the most powerful guys in the music business, I would have dismissed it. I had to remind myself these were also the same people who wanted to drop the Fugees after the first record. But that was then, and this is now. Circumstances were different, and the stakes could not be higher.

Besides this record being one of the most anticipated records in the music industry, this record also represented to Ruffhouse an important milestone from a financial perspective. It was the first record under our latest renegotiation with Sony (the co-venture) where the profits were to be split 50/50. This was significant since the co-venture profit split was not applicable to any of the artists already signed to Ruffhouse except Ms. Hill. This was a deal point Sony conceded to earlier on. Simply put, should this record be successful, Ruffhouse stood to make not just hundreds of thousands of dollars, but millions.

I went outside, lit a cigarette, and walked the streets of Bath until dawn. I kept walking until I was able sort out my thoughts and self-doubt. I walked miles through Bath's cobblestone streets, watching bakery vans and dairy trucks make predawn deliveries and cab drivers hanging out having animated conversations about English football. I had not had a sojourn this side of midnight, sober and drug free, in some time.

I thought of the events leading up to this moment. After I flew to Jamaica last year and met with Ms. Hill, I got on the plane coming back with the knowledge that the situation between Clef and her looked irreparable. She made it quite clear she was ready to do her own thing. A few weeks later, I had a barbeque at my house in Gladwyne. I invited Ms. Hill and her family to come over, but I did not really expect her to come. She had a new baby, and I thought her driving the hour and a half from South Orange to my house for a pool party was not at the top of her priority list. I offered to send my driver with my limo to pick her up. I was a little surprised when her mother, Valerie, called me and said they were coming. I sent Chuck, our driver, to go get them that Saturday morning.

When they showed up, we hung out with the other guests for a little while, and then we went to what Myrna and I called our music room, a room with large floor-to-ceiling windows looking out onto the back of my property. We had all of our records, CDs, and various musical instruments there—guitars, amps, mandolins, keyboards, etc. We sat down, and she started to tell me her vision for the new album.

In a period of roughly an hour, she described how she wanted to create a record embodying old-school recording techniques with live instrumentation. This was different as hip-hop, dance, and most pop music production was fast approaching the zenith of digital technology. Recording engineers in London had already started abandoning the use of multi-track two-inch tape recording. One engineer explained to me that it took too much time to wait for rewinds, especially when mixing. Now it was more about replacing live instrumentation with replicated samples. Ms. Hill described a recording process where the record would sound organic, like something recorded in the '60s and '70s. I could not have been more thrilled. After we talked, Chuck took Valerie, Ms. Hill, and baby Zion back to South Orange.

The following Monday morning, we set about submitting the budget requests to Sony Music for the project. Album budget requests were a standard procedure, not unlike other business transactions. You asked a corporation for money, and they wanted to know what and how you were going to spend it. Although there were no real rules, most R&B budgets in the eighties were about $120,000 for an album project, while rock and pop projects were in the $200,000–$300,000 range. In the early nineties, those budgets changed with the profitability of the business and overall inflation. But even though black music, especially hip-hop, was dominating the charts, there was still an unjustified disparity between what white artists and black artists were given. It was not until the mid-to-late nineties that there was a shift in that paradigm, not from some moral awakening by the majors, but due to actual production necessity.

The initial budget for Ms. Hill's album was probably about $1.5 million. She formed a holding company called Obverse Creations, and we started disbursing monies. There were no illusions about the record being recorded at Ruffhouse's Studio 4 facility in Conshohocken. With Ms. Hill being a new mother, it did not make sense logistically. Besides, once Ruffhouse artists reached a certain level of success, they tended to record in studios close to where they lived.

Sony had their own ideas on how they wanted to see this record get made. They obviously wanted Clef to be involved, but there was no way that was going to happen. If Clef was involved, I think it would have ended up being a Fugees album minus Pras, and Ms. Hill needed to do her own gig.

The Sony-nominated producers were all nonstarters. Ms. Hill wanted to make this record on her own, and she wanted to make a record using organic components. I do not remember how long the initial sessions were in New York and New Jersey, but she spent more time in Jamaica where she started recording at the famed Tuff Gong Studios. The record incorporated the same musical configuration as the Fugees records, but sonically it had a vintage analog warmth and richness. I was given the first few songs, which I immediately loved. I just wanted the world to hear it.

I thought it would ship a million copies and then sell through and then keep selling over time. My expectations may have been modest, but I was looking at this (as I am sure Ms. Hill was, as well) as an album project not relying on a schedule of singles. I had always had a '60s and '70s FM rock marketing mentality. Then, FM rock albums sold, regardless of what songs a major record label pushed, because FM rock stations played the songs they liked. Singles were important, but if the album itself had a weak musical narrative then there was no point. I always looked at albums as a conceptual snapshot of an artist's repertoire at that particular time period in his performing career. But the music business in the nineties was a tough place to build a career as a performing artist without having radio singles. As a result, the producers became almost more important than the artist, especially in a radio-driven genre like hip-hop and R&B.

The irony was that black artists of the '60s and '70s were

always shortchanged on album budgets, but now R&B producers with track records could command up $150,000 a song
while an entire rock record of 12 to 14 songs costs $300,000 to
$400,000.

Ms. Hill's album slowly but surely came together. I loved the
song "Ex-Factor," and after listening to it a few times, I thought
the verses ran too long. I actually thought she should cut the
first verse in half. She sings the verse and there is an expecta-
tion for the chorus to happen, but instead she takes you into
the verse again like she is making you wait. I brought this up
with her, and her response was to suggest that, by waiting, it is
more dramatic and powerful when it happens. After a few listens, I realized she was right. With the skits between the songs
and the album title, *The Miseducation of Lauryn Hill*, she presented an almost cinematographic storyline where the listener
became fully invested in the album rather than cursory listens
to the album tracks that accompany the highlighted radio singles. This was a true concept record. The album as a body of
work was raw but elegant and definitely a hip-hop record.

I had to come to admire Ms. Hill over the years, above and
beyond the fact she was a world-acclaimed artist. This record
went beyond just a solo endeavor by a member of a popular
group. The first time I met the Fugees in David Sonenberg's
office in New York City's Upper East Side, Ms. Hill did not
make the impression on me that Wyclef did as it appeared he
was the de facto leader and spokesperson of the group. During
the production of the first album, *Blunted on Reality*, I talked
with Wyclef and David almost daily. It was not until we shot the
first video for the song "Boof Baf" from that album that I had
my first real conversation with her.

Since signing the Fugees to Ruffhouse, I learned of her
pre-Fugees accomplishments, including her performance in

Sister Act 2. She wowed all of Hollywood with her performance in the film. At the video shoot, she told me she was a student at Columbia University, and she implied the Fugees were not the only priority in her life. She was planning on continuing her education. I thought that was going to be a challenge. This solo album represented for her not just a professional and creative departure from the Fugees but also a personal proclamation as an artist.

Life presented other challenges to Ms. Hill after the Fugees' tsunami of success engulfed the world. During an interview on *The Howard Stern Show*, Howard asked her a question regarding the success of *The Score* album. She answered with a remark having to do with the demographics of the audience and how she was appreciative of the mass crossover success of *The Score*, but she was concerned about the group maintaining their credibility among the core black audience as well. This was an intelligent and legitimate observation. We, as a label, had this discussion almost daily. But what happened next was completely misconstrued. A caller on the show said it sounded like, "Lauryn would rather kill her babies than sell records to white people."

Suddenly, out of the mouth of every idiot walking the face of God's gray earth came this hideous mantra: "Lauryn Hill is a racist! I heard her on *Howard Stern* saying she would kill her babies rather than have white people listen to or buy her music!"

It was so absurd, especially when people seemed to say it as though it was this fashionable affectation of PC propaganda. To this day, I still sometimes hear it from strangers at the mention of her name. It took years for me to learn to give up and not respond. But even this was not enough to quell the anticipation for millions of fans across the globe for this record.

In Bath, I walked back to the hotel after sunrise while Myrna was still asleep. I took a shower and told Myrna I would meet her downstairs for breakfast. I took the five songs and listened to them on headphones in the lobby. It seemed every time I listened to songs from this record I was reinvigorated with confidence and excitement. We flew back to Philadelphia on British Air a few days later.

Wyclef's *The Carnival* album went on to sell millions of copies worldwide and was a major success, so at the time, I was not really caring what people thought of the record. The tracks were assembled, but when it came time to do artwork there was another obstacle with Sony. Sony wanted a sexy photo, like a typical '90's R&B record for the cover. How they thought that would work with the title she chose, *The Miseducation of Lauryn Hill* was beyond me. Ms. Hill wanted to have a schoolroom theme in the CD gatefold pull out and a rendering on the front cover. Ms. Hill called me when I was in the middle of an interview with the *New York Times*. They were interviewing me for a business piece on Ruffhouse. She was upset that Sony was resistant to her concept of a rendering after I told them we were not using a photo on the cover. I assured her that they would get over it.

The writer for the *New York Times* wrote in the article that she surmised I was talking to Ms. Hill and quoted my words when I said something to the effect that the Sony guys were in the corporate culture. One Sony exec who read the article was not happy and told me so the next day. When I saw the proofs for the artwork, I could not have been more excited as I thought it was genius. The cover was the top of an antique school desk, like the ones I sat in as a kid in Catholic school. These old desks were designed to open, so you could store your composition book, your ruler, your pencils, and glue stick inside. The top of the desk had an indentation carved out where you kept your pencil, so it did not roll off. The title was etched in the desk at the top, and there was a carved rendering of Ms. Hill that looked beautiful, classic, and original. I believed once people at Sony saw this, any ideas regarding a photograph would be quickly forgotten.

The cover reminded me of the cover for Bob Marley and the Wailers' *Burnin'*, which came out in 1972. It was a rendering of the group made to look like it was burnt into wood. I loved the cover and was immensely proud of it.

I set about putting together a marketing plan by going over to Ms. Hill's house in South Orange. She had bought a very beautiful house she shared with her parents. She had gotten rid of her manager and was at this point doing this on her own. I went back to the methodology of selling records that I used with Schoolly D. My idea had always been straightforward and simple. If the record as a body of work is good and it's not just a collection of album cuts accompanying some designated singles, then it's a matter of people knowing about it. With Schoolly D, we had no radio singles, yet, independently, we sold over 300,000 records.

At this point, Ms. Hill had already sold twenty million-plus Fugees records worldwide, so the market had been established. "Doo Wop," the first single, made sense, but Ms. Hill and I came up with something that people in the business said was genius, but at the time it pissed a lot of people off at Sony. The opening track on the album, after the skit featuring the schoolroom roll call, is a song called "Lost Ones."

We hatched a plan to do a white label release independently. Sony did not know about it as it would take away the purpose of doing it to begin with. Two weeks before the release of the album, we shipped 1,000 copies of "Lost Ones" to mix show

DJs across the country and in the United Kingdom. It is a hard-hitting hip-hop track with a reggae dancehall flavor. It had an infectious beat, and Ms. Hill was on fire with her delivery.

The first call I got was from Pras who told me it was the most genius marketing and promotion he had ever witnessed. Then, I got a call from Michael Mauldin, who was head of the black music department at Sony. He was not happy about his department being left out of the loop. He warned me that Donnie would blow up my phone, but Donnie never did. The reason was I was sure people were calling him telling him what a great maneuver it was. I did get a call from Donnie right before the release of the album asking if I would agree to Sony raising the retail price of the CD from $19.99 to $20.99. I agreed. One dollar did not seem consequential for a record that would go on to change hip-hop.

CHAPTER TWELVE

AFTER THE GOLD RUSH

T*he Miseducation of Lauryn Hill* was released in August of
1998 and was the first album by a female to enter the
Billboard chart at the number one position. It sold
close to half a million copies over the counter in the
first week. The biggest challenge was the onslaught of
press, which was ravenous. We went to London and did a massive press conference, as well as select interviews with some of
the more important magazines and television shows. At this
point Ms. Hill was pregnant with her second child, making
this trip especially arduous. The reception of the album
among the fans was something beyond anything I had yet to
experience. The throngs of kids who fawned over Kris Kross
during their massive tours and appearances were one thing,

but this was a whole new level. What struck me was how this record seemed to touch every generation.

I jumped into a cab in London, and the track "Doo Wop" was playing on the stereo. I assumed it was the radio, which was no real surprise as radio in London was very pop, and the stations played everything. They did not have multiformat programming at the time in England. The stations played the current hit songs, no matter what genre. You could hear a Fugees song followed by an Oasis song, and so forth. There was no black radio format. However, there were influential DJs who had their own playlists. The cab driver was in his mid-sixties, and when "Doo Wop" ended and "Superstar" played, I realized he was listening to a CD. I asked him about it, and he said he had just bought it and had been listening to it nonstop. He also had *The Score* and *The Carnival* CDs, which he bought after he purchased the *Mis-Ed* CD. He said these were the only hip-hop CDs he owned and the rest of his music collection was rock and jazz.

Ms. Hill was on the cover of *Time* magazine as the figurehead for an article about how big hip-hop had become and how it was considered to be its own defined genre, along with rock, country, classical, R&B, and jazz. At that moment, Ruffhouse was considered one of the top purveyors of this newly recognized phenomenon.

There was also something else happening at the time for Ruffhouse that was significant: The company's contractual agreement with Sony was coming to an end.

I had a great relationship with Donnie Ienner at Sony, but I was not so sure about Tommy Mottola. Ms. Hill was scheduled to go to Japan, where she was scheduled to perform at a special event for the heads of Sony Corporation. I was scheduled to go with her. After this event was planned, I received a phone call from Tommy's office saying that Tommy wanted me to come up for a meeting with him and Danny DeVito about a Jersey Films project. The date for the meeting was on the same day as Ms. Hill's scheduled performance in Japan for Sony. I told Tommy's assistant I was going to Japan with Ms. Hill. Tommy's assistant went on to tell me how important this meeting was and how Tommy really wanted me to be there. So, I acquiesced and canceled my trip to Japan. Months earlier, after I did a TV interview on CNBC about the hip-hop business, I received a strange phone call from an executive at Columbia Records.

This executive went on to tell me how I was endangering my relationship with Tommy by doing press. I knew this executive, and while he talked to me, I thought his whole demeanor was very uncharacteristic. I suspected he was sitting in front of Tommy because he said things like, "Tommy should be the one talking to the press." When I told Kevon Glickman about my scheduled meeting with Danny DeVito and Tommy and how I had to cancel my trip to Japan, Kevon responded with an exasperated chuckle. I did not get it.

"I will bet you a hundred bucks the meeting gets canceled after Ms. Hill's plane takes off," Kevon said. I did not want to believe this, but, low and behold, the day after the scheduled departure for Japan and the night before the scheduled meeting with Tommy and Danny DeVito, Tommy's office called and canceled the meeting.

"Danny had to do some reshoots on a production and needs to reschedule."

The entire thing could be interpreted as somebody did not want me going to Japan and talking to the press, but I will never know for sure.

Up to this point, all of my dealings with Sony were with

Donnie, and I was very happy with the partnership. But at this point I thought it was going to be difficult to move ahead with Joey. I think he just wanted to be in the studio and did not want the responsibility of managing a label.

The simple truth was that I would have traded places with Joe any day of the week. To be able to come in, make records for other companies, and get paid as a co-owner of one of the biggest hip-hop labels in the world? Who would not want that gig? I did not begrudge him in the least. There was not anything said between us, but a few times he said things to other people that I found actually very hurtful. A lot of it centered around press.

Ruffhouse was a real player in this game, and the press wanted to talk about it. I did not solicit this. I was at Sony one day when I got a call saying one of the senior editors of *Vibe* magazine wanted to meet with me. We set up a time to meet at Nobu for drinks. I called my publicist to meet me there. The restaurant was surrounded by limousines and Lincoln Navigators. I went in and met the editor. We sat down, and within five minutes, he was showing off a diamond wrist bracelet given to him by either Andre Harrell or Puffy. This led to the mention of other gifts from label heads, mainly very expensive jewelry. The implication was not so subtle to be lost on me. If I wanted coverage in *Vibe*, I needed to drop some coin at Harry Winston. I thought it was completely absurd. We went upstairs, and within a few minutes, I found myself in a very animated conversation with future president Donald Trump.

Donald was apparently friends with a lot of the big hip-hop artists and went on to tell me that he was also very good friends with Russell Simmons. I found him to be a very amicable guy. He congratulated me repeatedly on the success of the company. I was called on the phone the next morning saying my encounter with Trump was mentioned in the *New York Daily News*. I did not solicit that moment.

The press I received only fueled speculation about the future of the label. I had a meeting with Donnie who proposed I take over RED distribution and become a Sony executive. I was initially excited about this and even started to think about getting a house in Connecticut or moving into NYC as Myrna and I did not have children. The idea was intriguing in that I would run one of the biggest independent distributors, and I would report directly to Donnie.

Not surprisingly, Tommy nixed the idea, as I think he did not want to see Donnie getting any more powerful than he was. But there was also a forthcoming event that would change everything.

The *Mis-Ed* album was nominated for a staggering ten Grammy Awards, which was the most amount of nominations for a female artist in the history of the Grammys. Popular music culture had Lauryn Hill on the brain, and there was no stopping it. I would be lying if I said I was not going to use this situation to raise the stakes. The Grammys were being held in L.A. I booked the L'Eermitage in Beverly Hills, where I had been staying as of late. As it turned out, Ms. Hill and her family were also staying there, so it worked out quite nicely. And Kevon had set up some meetings while we were out there. I had a number of major labels interested in bringing me over to create a new company.

We went to EMI chairman Ken Berry's house to meet with him about coming over to EMI. I was interested at the time, but I also wanted to hear what two other companies had to say. Paul Schindler from the Grubman firm had set up a meeting with David Geffen. David had set up a new company with Steven Spielberg and Jeffrey Katzenberg, called DreamWorks. It was a new major motion picture studio with an adjoining record company. The record company was run by Mo Ostin, another industry legend who had started with Reprise Records and gone on to head Warner Brothers Records.

I first had a meeting with David Geffen at his house in Beverly Hills. I drove a rental car to the address, which I found painted on the curb in front of a long line of hedgerow. But there was no driveway, just the address numbers painted on the curb like they do in L.A. I sat in the car, and after about three minutes, the hedgerow opened up, revealing a guardhouse. An attendant approached the car wearing a windbreaker and a Desert Eagle handgun. (This was not long after the assassination of Gianni Versace, so it was understandable.) The house was formerly the estate of Jack Warner, and David's purchase of it was at the time the largest private purchase of a home in U.S. history. I drove up an approach road that went for at least a mile into the courtyard of a beautiful mansion. I had lunch with David, and he took me on a tour of the house, showing me his art collection, which I was later told was worth three hundred million dollars.

After a short tour of the grounds outside, David walked me to my car, and I left. The entire visit seemed like it was choreographed to the minute. It was a very impressive presentation of power and very effective. I could not see how anybody would not want to be in business with this guy after an encounter like this. I found out later he did not even live in this house but spent his time at a beach house in Malibu. He only used this house for meetings and parties. It was quite an experience to meet the most powerful guy in the music business and, arguably, the richest. I met with Mo Ostin at the DreamWorks Records office the next day, which happened to be located behind the L'Eermitage.

It was a great meeting; Robbie Robertson, member of the iconic rock group the Band, was there. He was now a Dream-Works Music executive. I had a meeting scheduled the next day with the chairman of Warner Brothers Records, which I was admittedly very excited about. That night was the Grammys, and Ms. Hill's ten nominations were the talk of the town. She won five Grammys, beating the record for the most Grammys won by a female artist for a single album since Carole King's *Tapestry*. It was an amazing time, especially when Ms. Hill specifically thanked me every time she accepted. But the biggest moment was when Sting announced Ms. Hill as the winner for the album of the year.

This was the culmination of everything that had happened since the day I left for the Navy in the winter of 1977.

The Sony party later that night was different from all the others I had attended. For me, it was very surreal, not only because I had an artist win for a record that impacted the world but I also felt a new confidence in what I was doing. I was clean, sober, and I felt vindicated, and I was ready to do more, which is why I was excited for my meeting at Warner Brothers the next day.

I had always been fascinated with Warner Brothers, and not just the label, but the entire company. I remember as a kid looking at the actual vinyl album center labels depicting Olive Avenue in Burbank with the palm trees on each side. The day of the meeting, Kevon and I went over to Warner Brothers in Burbank. The record company was located next to the movie studio lot. We met with Russ Thyret, the chairman of the company, and it was really great. I liked EMI and DreamWorks, but I had an idea: I wanted to be the guy to bring black music back to Warner Brothers Music.

Next to Disney, Warner Brothers was one of the last American-owned entertainment conglomerates, but, at this point, it was considered a West Coast rock label. Its last successful forays into black music were Prince and Ice-T. I thought, with Warner's existing structure as a major distribution power, I could introduce the existing Ruffhouse DNA into it, and it could all come together. But I was not ready to make a decision yet until I could see what kind of commitment I'd receive from all three labels (EMI, WB, and DreamWorks).

This was going to be a process, and I wasted no time in getting the show together. I had put together a complete business plan completely broken down with budgets and projections. We had initiated serious conversations, but the first order of business was to get the Ruffhouse/Sony situation taken care of.

Sony did make me an offer to stay, but it did not make any real sense compared to my current market value as a label. Joe and I had separate attorneys representing us for the sale of the artist contracts to Sony. The negotiations went back and forth for about two months until, finally, Sony made an offer to buy out the Ruffhouse artist contracts; that even surprised the people at Grubman. It was an eight-figure sum—enough for Joe and me to sail off into the sunset. I received the offers from the three labels. EMI and WB were almost the same, but DreamWorks's offer was very light. I called Mo Ostin, and he said that DreamWorks did not own their own distribution, like EMI and WB, so they were not positioned to make a comparable offer.

In April of 1999, I ended up going with Warner Brothers.

Joe and I were not going to give each other the use of the Ruffhouse name. It was at that point a very valuable asset. As a matter of fact, for me to even use the name RuffNation, I needed to come to an accommodation with Joe. It was explained to me that I could run into legal issues with Joe over the name. Conceivably, by incorporating the "Ruff" in the name, I would be looked at as having diluted the value of the Ruffhouse brand, which was the last remaining jointly owned asset of the Ruffhouse partnership. I ended up buying his share of the name years later. People really seemed to dig the name RuffNation. We ended up moving to new offices in Bryn Mawr, Pennsylvania, not far from where I lived. I built a world-class recording studio. Joe did a deal with RCA and called his new label Judgment Records. Although we did not talk for a long time, we eventually saw each other, and no grudges were held.

Going to Warner Brothers was exciting at first. Although the deal was beset with problems from the very start, I felt we made some impact in a short amount of time. We had signed a group from Newark, New Jersey, called the Outsidaz. We were originally introduced to them via the Fugees, as they participated in some of the Fugees' production. This deal had come about via Method Man and Redman who put the Outsidaz on their tour. The "Outs," as we called them, had a lot of promise, especially members Pacewon and Young Zee. We decided to start with an EP, which we would release though our independent label, Rufflife, which would be marketed through Warner's independent arm ADA (Alternative Distribution Alliance). The EP did very well. It featured Eminem on one song, and he also appeared in the video we shot at city hall in Philadelphia. The tour with Method Man and Redman ended prematurely when one of the Outsidaz's members struck a security guard at the House of Blues in Chicago. They were kicked off the tour. This was after I had wrapped a tour bus with the artwork from the EP and bought a Vari-Light system. The Vari-Light allowed me to project images like logos fifty feet high onto the sides of buildings. Still, the EP did very well, and we started an album project. I also signed a group from Philadelphia called Major Figgas, who were sought after by every major label. The challenge was every group member had a solo deal on another label, and as a result, there were six or seven different managers involved. The record was not successful, as I feel we had rushed it out. I also signed an R&B group from Philadelphia called No Question. They were signed to Philadelphia International Records and had a hit song on the radio called "I Don't Care." Through their managers, Vance DeBose and Khan Jamal, I did a deal with Kenny Gamble to put the record through the RuffNation/Warners distribution. I also signed a singer named Leela James. We did a fantastic record with her. I did a soundtrack album for a Jamie Foxx film called *Bait*, directed by Antoine Fuqua. Although the movie did not do so well at the box office, we had a number one single by Interscope Recording artist Mya. The song was called "Free" and was produced by Jimmy Jam and Terry Lewis. But I had some unforeseen challenges with Warner Brothers Records. The parent company, Time-Warner, did a deal with AOL shortly after we had come on board that proved to be disastrous for stockholders. Chairman Gerald Levin ended up stepping down. I cannot say this was a result of that, but there was suddenly a wave of executive changes, which eventually saw Russ Thyret, the head of the record division, leave the company. We had delivered records, had artists on tour, and were in full swing when suddenly there was no label head at Warners. It seemed like everything stopped unless it was an established Warner Brothers artist. At one point, I was told by a department head at Warner Brothers Records that nobody wanted to spend any money or do anything until there was a clear picture of who was coming in.

By the time that happened, we had lost significant momentum. Once a record gets released through major distribution, it needs to sell through in a short amount of time. Looking back, what I should have done was release everything independently through the Warners ADA distribution first, not just a few select projects. Some of the artists, like Major Figgas, I believe would have benefited from allowing us to seed the marketplace first. But this is something I should have figured out beforehand. I was just too anxious to make a splash at the time.

But, during all of this, there was a monumental event for Myrna and me: the birth of my daughter, Ava, on November 21, 2000. Regardless of what was happening at the company, I was over-the-top thrilled with having a child. Myrna and I held off doing this for years for two reasons. First, although I could run a multi-million-dollar company, I did not have my shit together enough to become a father. The years of drug abuse would not have made a suitable environment for raising a child. Second, I considered myself too busy. I realized later that there is never a good time in that regard.

After the dust cleared with Warner Bros., I went to work with Sony Music as consultant. During this time, I produced a number of feature films with Rich Murray. Our first film, *Snipes*, starred Zoe Saldana, Nelly, and Frank Vincent. Later, in 2011, I did a deal with EMI label services releasing a record by Philadelphia hip-hop artist Beanie Sigel. Beanie was previously signed to Jay Z's Roc-A-Fella Records. He had some big records with his group State Property. He also did a film produced by Roc-A-Fella partner Damon Dash called *State Property* which was an independent gangster film shot in Philadelphia. It did very well for an independent release. Beanie was considered by hip-hop backpack aficionados to be one of hip-hop's true street poets. I do not disagree. Although Beanie and his crew are from Philly, we had never crossed paths before, so I did not really know him. We met, and he played me around

15–16 songs in the studio. He said he owned everything, including the publishing. The tracks just needed to be mixed. We mixed the songs at Studio 4, the original Ruffhouse studio, with Phil Nicolo, Joey's twin brother. After we delivered the record to EMI with the artwork, they set about manufacturing for an August 12, 2012 release date, ending a twelve-year hiatus for Ruffhouse Records. Shortly after we released the record, Beanie had asked me to meet him at his lawyers' office downtown. I was not sure what this meeting was about. I knew he had some tax issues. It was at this meeting that I learned his "tax issues" were monumental. His lawyers told me Beanie had pleaded guilty to income tax evasion months before and they were awaiting sentencing, which they had been pushing back. I was feeling beyond distraught. I did not know what to do. The record came out the day of sentencing. We wrote letters to the judge, but there was no way he would be dissuaded. The prosecutor wanted to send a message to hip-hop artists. The judge, however, did give Beanie eight weeks to do promotion before he would have to report to jail. That night he was arrested for being in a car with some other people with a gun. We had a number of radio interviews, shows, and a performance on *Jimmy Kimmel Live!* set up, but everything went down the drain. Given the situation, I believe if he did not get arrested that night, we could have salvaged the situation. If I had known he had already pleaded guilty and was just awaiting sentencing, I would have approached the entire project differently or maybe not have done it at all. But I was not given that choice. After the whole Beanie debacle, I would spend the next few years working on different productions, and I am now setting up an entirely new distribution platform.

Recently, Joe and I were awarded the Philadelphia Music

Alliance's "Walk of Fame" award, a bronze plaque on the sidewalk in Philadelphia among plaques awarded to everybody from Hall and Oates, Will Smith, Gamble and Huff, and others. After the unveiling ceremony, the Philadelphia Music Alliance hosted a gala dinner for us in Philadelphia. Joe and his family and Myrna, Ava, and I all sat together at a table for the awards. It was a really great event, and it was awesome hanging out with Joe for the first time in eighteen years, along with Schoolly D, who presented the award to us. I realized that night we had put out records by almost fifty artists over a period of time. I do not know where my life would have gone if I had not wanted as a kid to be a musician so badly. I often think that if I had the musical chops, I would not have ended up in the record business. The music business has always been and will always be an incredibly difficult business. We were amazingly successful, and it is truly remarkable what can happen if you want something bad enough. You must be willing to step into the unknown.

ACKNOWLEDGMENTS

WHILE I AM an avid reader of books, I never realized just how much went into the creation of a book beyond the writing. The publication of this book would not have been possible without the help and encouragement of many people who spent a great deal of time, effort, energy, and resources to bring it to fruition. Many thanks to my agent, Adrienne Rosado at Stonesong, who saw the potential of this project early and devoted her time so generously. Thanks to Diversion Books's publisher, Scott Waxman, who gave me the chance to tell my story. Thanks to the team at Diversion Books, who have shown nothing but enthusiasm, including my editor, Mark Weinstein, who helped me immensely to make the narrative flow, freelance developmental editor Katherine Benoit Cardoso, copyeditor Katie Swift, project editor Jeff Farr of Neuwirth & Associates, publicist Lissa Warren, cover designer Bret Kerr, and acquiring editor Lia Ottaviano. Special thanks to Brilliance Audio. Extra special thanks to Kay Vaughn, who got the ball rolling! I also want to thank my wife, Myrna, for keeping me in check throughout all the good and bad, and my daughter, Ava, who makes me proud every day. I'd also like to thank my newly discovered daughter, Sommer Spillane, and her family, with whom I could not be happier we connected. Special thanks to the Jordans: Bobby, Caroline & Sophie. Thanks to my cousin, Missy Schwartz, who is always there for me and my sister, Meg Wood, who always encouraged me. Special thanks to Joe Nicolo, Phil Nicolo, Rose Mann, Jesse "Schoolly D" Weaver,

Ahmir "Questlove" Thompson, Laiya St. Clair, Zarah Zohlman, Cara Lewis, Jeremy Holgersen, Pete Dolnak, Walt Beach, Luc & Donna Vergier, Jerry Duplessis, Warren Hamilton, Jeff Coulter, Rich Murray, Kevon Glickman, Ian Cross, Randy Cantor, Walt Bass, Rob Dippold, Dave Janofsky, Glenn Manko, Kevin Bass, Jeff Wells, Robert "Big Bob" Crippen, Tamara Feldman, Stefanie Lock Wielgus, Andy Kravitz, Arthur Mann, Kurt Woodley, Vance DeBose, Khan Jamal, Chris Blackwell, Will Smith, Helen Little, Todd Wolfe, Josh Boumel, Cozmic Kev, Randy Cantor, Michael Caruso, Dave Mays, Chris Robinson, Joe Rey, Terry Akins, Larry Gold, Alan Grunblatt, Barry Weiss, Paul Schindler, Don Ienner, John Ingrassia, Fred Ehrlich, Jeff Walker, Tom Mackay, Rob Stringer, Jerry Blair, Deirdre O'Hara, Rick Chertoff, Rob Hyman, Dave Uosikkinen, Steven Rifkind, Lyor Cohen, Peter Malkin, Jimmy Iovine, Bryan Turner, Tom Mackay, David Kahne, Johnny Coppola, Nasty Nes, Dennis Lavinthal, Lenny Beer, Monte Lipman, Craig Davis, Robin White, Lydell Russell, Cara Lewis, Colleen Theis, Howard Wulfing, Marc Ghuneim, Denny Somach, Susan Blond, Steve Barnett, David Sonenberg, Faith Newman, Charlie Walk, Angela Thomas, Camille Yorrick, Suzette Williams, Commissioner Williams, Warren Reicher, Kenny Gamble, Leon Huff, Chuck Gamble & The PIR Family, Alan Rueben, Randy Alexander, The Philadelphia Music Alliance, Funk Master Flex, Marley Marl, Red Alert, Kid Capri, DJ Khalid, John Kolodner, Daryl Hall, John Oates, Dave Johnson, Clare Godholm, Andy Kravitz, Doug Grigsby, Rhythm of Lines, John Doelp, Bob Calagiuri, Evan Gusz, AD Amoroso, Dave Jurman, Michael Mauldin, Happy Walters, Amanda Scheer, Mio Vukovic, Jeff Fenster, Len Fico, Michael Caruso, Tom Tierney, Paula Erickson, Toby Silver, Che Williams, Danny Lee, John Saachi, Matt Groesch, Madeline Nelson, Dre

& Vidal, Carvin & Ivan, Jazzy Jeff, James Posner and all of my friends at Columbia Records/Sony Music, Warner Bros., EMI, Universal, and E One. The Orchard, RED, Fontana, ADA. WMA, CAA, UTA, Endeavor. Heartfelt thanks go out to all of the artists, especially Ms. Lauryn Hill and the Hill Family, Wyclef Jean, Prakazrel "Pras" Michel, Lawrence "Muggs" Muggerud, Louis "B-Real" Frees, Senen "Sen Dog" Reyes, Eric Bobo, Chris Smith, Nasir "Nas" Jones, Jermaine Dupri, DMX, Beanie Sigel, State Property, Kool Keith, The Goats, Dandelion, Psycho Realm, Call O' Da Wild, Leela James, Mac Money & DJ QST, Robbie B & DJ Jazz, Tidewater Grain and to all of the other Ruffhouse & RuffNation artists: Josh Wink, King Britt, Sporty Thieves, Liz Leite, Jamie Myerson, Jason Jordan, Vincent Carol, Whey Cooler, Chrissy Pergolini, Keith Martin, Maja Figgas, The OutSidaz, Trip 66, Cam, Blackmale, No Question, Voices of Theory, Ski, James King, Paul Murray, Glenn Lewis, The Mountain Brothers, Armand Van Helden, Kulcha Don, Tuff Crew, and Larry Larr. In memoriam: Chris "Mac Daddy" Kelly, Timothy "Tim Dog" Blair, Tony D, Larry Schwartz, Richard Nichols, Todd 1, Melvin Wallace, Frank Virtue, Richard Barrett, Lisa Campbell, Charlie Kountz, Ricky Leigh Mench, Jeff Wells, David Reilly, and Cheba. Big thanks to everybody at radio and retail, and to all of the fans who have supported these artists. Shout out to my friends at Ardmore, Chapman, and Conicelli.

ABOUT THE AUTHOR

CHRIS SCHWARTZ is the co-founder of Ruffhouse Records. Throughout the 1990s, Ruffhouse was home to some of the biggest names in hip-hop, including the Fugees, Ms. Lauryn Hill, Wyclef Jean, Cypress Hill, Nas, Kris Kross, DMX, Beanie Sigel, State Property, Schoolly D, and others. Ruffhouse Records sold over 120 million records worldwide, generating over a billion dollars in sales and earning a multitude of Grammy Awards. Chris has been the recipient of many awards celebrating his success, including 250 gold and platinum records.

Chris has been recognized in numerous national and international publications including the *Wall Street Journal*, the *New York Times*, *Los Angeles Times*, *Forbes*, *Rolling Stone*, *Vibe*, *Billboard*, *The Source*, *Variety*, *The Hollywood Reporter*, *Entertainment Weekly*, and *Vanity Fair*. He has also made TV appearances on CNN, CNN-FN, MSNBC, BBC, MTV, BET, and VH1.

The recipient of the National Association of Recording Arts and Sciences Governor's Award, The Dyana Williams Lifetime Achievement Award, and the Philadelphia Music Alliance "Walk of Fame" Award, Chris has been a guest speaker at University of Pennsylvania's Wharton School of Business, Drexel University, St. Joseph's University, Temple University, The Philadelphia Academy of the Arts, and the Philadelphia College of the Performing Arts.

Chris lives in Gladwyne, Pennsylvania, with his wife, Myrna, and daughter, Ava.

INDEX

INDEX

INDEX

CPSIA information can be obtained
at www.ICGtesting.com
Printed in the USA
BVHW070428150620
581447BV00002B/4